THE ULTIMATE
CAKE MIX & MORE
COOKBOOK

The paper in this printing meets the requirements of the ANSI Standard Z39.48-1992.

While every care has been taken in compiling the recipes for this book, the publisher, Cogin, Inc., or any other person who has been involved in working on this publication assumes no responsibility or liability for any errors or omissions, inadvertent or not, that may be found in the recipes or text, nor for any problems or damages that may arise as a result of preparing these recipes.

If food allergies or dietary restrictions are a concern, it is recommended that you carefully read ingredient product labels as well as consult a nutritionist or your physician to determine if a particular recipe meets your dietary needs.

We encourage you to use caution when working with all kitchen equipment and to always follow food safety guidelines.

To purchase this book for business or promotional use or to purchase more than 50 copies at a discount, or for custom editions, please contact Cogin, Inc. at the address below or info@mrfood.com.

Inquiries should be addressed to:
Cogin, Inc.
1770 NW 64 Street, Suite 500
Fort Lauderdale, FL 33309

ISBN: 978-0-9911934-8-6

Printed in the United States of America
First Edition

www.MrFood.com
Facebook.com/MrFoodRecipes
Twitter.com/Mr_Food
Instagram.com/MrFoodTestKitchen
YouTube.com/MrFoodVideos

Introduction

There's nothing like the feeling you get when you've just finished frosting a homemade cake or the smell of freshly baked cookies coming out of the oven. Baking is one of life's simple pleasures, which is why we've created the "The Ultimate Cake Mix & More Cookbook." This book makes it easy for anyone to make their favorite desserts without needing any fancy equipment or lots of ingredients. We've kept it simple, so that you enjoy your time in the kitchen as much as everyone enjoys the sweet results.

Why dig out all of those canisters filled with ingredients you only use once in a blue moon, when you can begin any creative dessert with a box of cake mix? A cake mix includes all of the basic ingredients you need to get that showstopping dessert started. And, oh yeah, in this cookbook we're giving you plenty of ideas to take your cake mixes, and even your brownie and cookie mixes, to a whole new level. There's nothing typical about these recipes! This cookbook is jam-packed with more than 130 quick and easy recipes that start with a mix and end up with homemade, bakery-worthy results.

No matter what the occasion, we've got a whole lot of desserts for you to choose from. If it's a potluck you've been invited to, then you're going to love our wide variety of bars, squares, brownies, and cupcakes that are easy to bake and take! And, if your family loves cake, whether it's been poked, "dumped," or baked in a Bundt pan, then you may have a hard time deciding which one to make first. Of course, we didn't forget about those decadent layer cakes that always turn heads – there's plenty of those recipes in here too! And for all the occasions that require something, maybe not-so-expected, we've included a chapter full of recipes for, "A Little of This, A Little of That."

What's the icing on top of the cake? Homemade frostings and glazes! (Yeah, we took that pretty literally.) It's hard not to go weak at the knees thinking about all the decadent goodness that awaits you. Once you start baking with these recipes, we know you'll agree that it's never been easier...or tastier.

So, whether you're just starting out in the kitchen or you're a seasoned pro, you'll love how quick and easy these recipes are. Finally, a book that will not only help you make incredible homemade-tasting desserts, but one that'll be a true memory maker. And with such sweet results, you can bet that everyone will swear your desserts were "made-from-scratch." Actually, you may not hear anything, except the satisfying sound of everyone saying,...

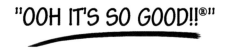

"OOH IT'S SO GOOD!!®"

**Other titles you may enjoy from the
Mr. Food Test Kitchen:**

Christmas Made Easy

Quick & Easy Comfort Cookbook

Sinful Sweets & Tasty Treats

Just One More Bite!

Hello Taste, Goodbye Guilt!

Cook it Slow, Cook it Fast

Guilt-Free Weeknight Favorites

Wheel of Fortune Collectible Cookbook

The Ultimate Cooking for Two Cookbook

As always, we remember our founder, Art Ginsburg, who believed that everyone would cook (and bake!) if only we could make it "quick & easy." We thank you for allowing us to carry on this tradition.

Table of Contents

Acknowledgements

Who would think that it would take so many people to create a cookbook? We sure wouldn't have if we hadn't worked on it ourselves. But the reality is that it does, and we are so thankful that we've assembled such a talented team over the years.

Patty Rosenthal
Test Kitchen Director

Howard Rosenthal
Chief Food Officer

Kelly Rusin
Photographer & Stylist

Merly Mesa
Editor

Jodi Flayman
Director of Publishing

Carol Ginsburg
Editor

Amy Magro
Dir. of Business Affairs

Jaime Gross
Business Assistant

Yolanda Reid
Brand Ambassador

Steve Ginsburg
Chief Executive Officer

Dave DiCarlo
Test Kitchen Assistant

Ana Cook
Website Editor

Roxana DeLima
Comptroller

Hal Silverman
Post Production
Hal Silverman Studio

Lorraine Dan
Book Design
Grand Design

Tips for Making Your Creations
Test Kitchen-Perfect:

Package Sizes:
As you're flipping through the book, you might notice that we didn't include the package sizes of boxed cake and brownie mixes in our recipes. There's a simple reason for that! We found that many of the national brands differ slightly in terms of package weight. To make sure that these slight differences would have no effect on the recipes, we tested a variety of brands. The good news is, they all yielded fantastic results! So, instead of causing you any confusion we thought it'd be easier for you to use whichever brand you prefer.

To Line or Not to Line:
If you want your cake to pop out easily from the pan, we often suggest placing a layer of wax or parchment paper on the bottom of the pan. Trim it, so it lays flat, then add your batter to the pan. Once it's baked, you can invert the cake and gently remove the paper.

To Spray or Not to Spray:
Always make sure that you read the directions carefully when it comes to coating a pan with cooking spray. Some recipes will suggest spraying the entire inside of the pan while others suggest that you only coat the bottom. The reason for that is, that if you coat the sides of a pan, the batter may have a hard time sticking to the sides during baking, which can interfere with the cake's ability to rise.

Crumb-Free Frosting:
We've got the secret to keeping crumbs out of your frosting. First, you need to let your cake cool. Then, brush off any loose crumbs with a pastry brush. Once this has been done, apply a very thin layer of frosting to "set" the crumbs. It doesn't matter if there are crumbs in this layer, since this is what is commonly known as a "crumb coat." After this layer has set, just apply a second layer of frosting and voila! You've got a perfect crumb-free frosting!

Beyond Food Color:

Since we eat with our eyes, adding liquid food color is a fun way to jazz up our cakes and frostings. But, if you're looking for a really rich or vibrant color, you might want to use liquid gel dyes or gel paste dyes. These are usually more intense and make it easier to get brighter reds, truer blues, and so on.

Bundt® or Ring:
Over the years, as the Bundt® pan found its way into the hearts and homes of people everywhere, the Bundt cake became a staple and a tradition for countless family gatherings and family celebrations, including the occasional Greek wedding (you did see the movie, didn't you?). Even though the Bundt pan is a registered trademark of the Nordic Ware® company, the name "Bundt" has become synonymous with almost any type of ring-shaped baking pan. No matter what you call it, we wish you nothing "Bundt" the best with all your baking! (Don't forget to check out the chapter, A Bounty of Bundts!)

Layered Cakes: Perfect Layers:

When you're cutting a layer cake in half, horizontally, the best way to ensure that it's cut evenly is to measure the halfway point on the cake cake, vertically, with a ruler and mark the cake at that point by partially inserting a toothpick in it. Continue marking all the way around the cake, about every 2-3 inches. Then, with a long serrated knife, cut the cake, using the toothpicks as a guide, while turning it. Remove the toothpicks and there you have it!

- Domed or Flat? That is the Question.

  When assembling a layer cake, you can choose to have a flat top or a domed one.

  - Domed Top: Trim the dome off only one of your two layers. Place the trimmed layer cut-side down on a platter. Frost the top of the first layer and place the second layer on top, dome-side up. Frost as directed.

  - Flat Top: Follow the directions above, except cut the dome off both cakes. The second layer should be placed above the frosted layer with the cut-side down.

Don't throw away the trimmings! You can use them to crumble over your finished cake as a decoration or you can enjoy them as a treat before the cake is ready to be eaten.

A What? A Poke Cake?:

If you're not familiar with poke cakes, it's about time you were introduced! A poke cake is simply a baked cake that has largish holes poked into it. The holes are then filled with anything and everything, from fruit preserves to fudgy sauces, which create "streams" of flavor throughout the cake. In case you're still a little confused, here are the basic steps:

1. Bake a cake in the designated pan, usually a 9- x 13-inch pan.
2. Poke lots of holes in the cake with the handle of a wooden spoon.
3. Pour filling over the cake and into the holes.
4. Spread the filling to allow it to fill into all of the holes.
5. Finish with topping or frosting.
6. Cut and enjoy!

We've got lots of poke cake recipes in the Pokes and Dumps chapter, with a wide variety of fillings and toppings. These cakes are so easy and so good, you might just find yourself doing the "hokey pokey"!

Cupcake Batter 101:
We've made lots of cupcakes in the Test Kitchen and we've found that the easiest way to divvy up the batter from the mixing bowl into the muffin cups is with an ice cream scoop.

Perfectly-Sized Cookies:
One of the keys to making good drop cookies is to make sure that they're all the same size. The best way to ensure that they're uniform is to use a small ice cream-type scoop to measure the dough. As a rule of thumb, a 1-ounce scoop will yield a 2-inch cookie. Remember, most cookies will spread, so leave some room between them. We suggest test-baking a few cookies for size before making a whole batch.

Is It Done Yet?:
One of the best ways to make sure a cake is baked through is to use the toothpick test. The test is easy! All you have to do is place a wooden toothpick in the center of the cake. If it comes out clean, it's done. If it has wet batter on it, then you should leave the cake in the oven to finish baking and retest after a few more minutes. We always recommend testing at the lower end of the range given, so if a recipe calls for a cake to bake for 25 to 30 minutes, then you should test it at 25 minutes. This test can be used for all types of cakes, from layer cakes to cupcakes.

Keeping Your Cake Stand Clean:
To keep your cake stand clean while frosting, line the edge with 3-inch strips of wax paper. Center the first cake layer over the strips. When you're finished frosting, carefully remove the strips one piece at a time.

Pour it On:
If you would like to make a quick glaze to drizzle over a cake or cupcakes, all you need to do is open a plastic can of store bought frosting, remove the foil, and microwave the container for several seconds, stirring it occasionally. When it's pourable, but not too hot, drizzle away.

Yikes, No Pastry Bag!:
If you want to add a bakery look to your baked goods, it's nice to have an inexpensive pastry bag and a few tips on hand. You can buy these at most markets or big box stores. If you find yourself in a pickle without one, all you need to do is fill a quart- or gallon-sized plastic storage bag with your frosting and, with scissors, cut off a small piece of one corner. Then, secure the top of the bag with your hands and gently add pressure. It's a quick-fix that gets the job done!

Gluten-Free...Yeah!:
Since so many of you have asked for more gluten-free recipes, we've created a number of them to include throughout this book. They're easy to spot too - just look for the words "Gluten Free" at the bottom of the recipe. When preparing these recipes, it's important to make sure that all of the ingredients used are gluten-free (just check the label!), especially if you're avoiding gluten due to health concerns. If you're not sure whether these recipes or any of the ingredients are right for you, you can always check with your healthcare professional.

Where Can I find It?:
Over the years many of you have asked where to find the bakeware we use in our Test Kitchen. If you would like to whip up your goodies in our new line of Mr. Food Test Kitchen bakeware and tableware, (see some of it on pages 62, 88, 124, 162, 184, and 228) simply go to www. MrFood.com and click on the "Shop" tab. We've got everything there from butter dishes and bakers, to serving trays and cookie jars.

Welcome to the Mr. Food Test Kitchen Family!

Whether you've been a fan of the Mr. Food Test Kitchen for years or were just recently introduced to us, we want to welcome you into our kitchen...and our family. Even though we've grown in many ways over the years, the one thing that hasn't changed is our philosophy for quick & easy cooking...and baking.

Over thirty years ago we began by sharing our recipes with you through the television screen. Today, not only is the Mr. Food Test Kitchen TV segment syndicated all over the country, but we've also proudly published over 50 best-selling cookbooks. That's not to mention the hugely popular MrFood.com and EverydayDiabeticRecipes.com. And for those of you who love to get social, we do too! You can find us online on Facebook, Twitter, Pinterest, and Instagram—boy, do we love connecting with you!

If you've got a passion for baking (like we do!), then you know that the only thing better than curling up with a cookbook and drooling over the pictures is actually getting to taste the finished recipes. That's why we give you simple step-by-step instructions that make it feel like we're in your kitchen guiding you along the way. Your taste buds will be celebrating in no time!

By the way, now that you're part of the family, we want to let you in on a little secret...we recently launched all sorts of tools and bakeware to make your life in the kitchen even easier. Be sure to let your friends and family know, 'cause once everyone gets word of it, we're not sure how long they'll stay on the shelves!

So whether you're new to the family or you've been a part of it from the beginning, we want to thank you. You can bet there is always room at our table for you, because there's nothing better than sharing in all of the..."OOH IT'S SO GOOD!!®"

Patty   Howard   Kelly

A Bounty of Bundts

Double Lemon Blueberry Bundt

Who can forget the classic scene from My Big Fat Greek Wedding when Maria Portokalos is given a Bundt cake and exclaims, "There's a hole in this cake!"? Thanks to her, most of us now know what Bundt cakes are. If for some crazy reason you're still not familiar with them, this super moist and lemony cake is a great one to start with. (We won't judge you if you decorate yours with a plant in the middle, like she did!)

Serves 12

Ingredients

1 package yellow cake mix, divided

1 cup fresh blueberries

1 [4-serving size] package instant lemon pudding mix

4 eggs

⅔ cup vegetable oil

⅔ cup water

1 cup confectioners' sugar

1 tablespoon lemon juice

Preparation

1 Preheat oven to 325 degrees F. Coat a Bundt pan with cooking spray. In a small bowl, toss 2 teaspoons cake mix with blueberries until evenly coated; set aside.

2 In a large bowl with an electric mixer, beat remaining cake mix, pudding mix, eggs, oil, and water until thoroughly combined. Stir blueberries into batter and pour into pan.

3 Bake 50 to 55 minutes, or until a toothpick comes out clean. Let cool 15 to 20 minutes, then invert onto a platter to cool completely.

4 Meanwhile, in a small bowl, whisk confectioners' sugar and lemon juice until smooth. Spoon glaze over cake and serve.

Did You Know? *The first official Bundt pan was created by Dave Dalquist, co-founder of Nordic Ware® bakeware, in 1950. It was a fluted cake pan made from cast aluminum. As the popularity of Bundt cakes grew, so did the demand for different styles. Today, we can find them in all sorts of designs, from the basic flute to fancier ones that resemble flowers, spirals, and even castles! You'll find some of these different designs in the Bundt cakes to follow.*

Cookies and Cream Bundt Cake

Over the years, we've used our favorite chocolate sandwich cookies to make everything from cookie crusts for cheesecakes to the perfect creamy milkshake. So, you can only imagine how excited we were when we successfully added them to this overstuffed, layered Bundt cake. It's amazing!

Serves 12

Ingredients

1 package dark chocolate cake mix

3 eggs

1 cup water

½ cup vegetable oil

2 tablespoons chocolate syrup

1 stick (½ cup) butter, softened

3 ounces cream cheese, softened

1 teaspoon vanilla extract

2-½ cups confectioners' sugar

2 tablespoons heavy cream

1 cup coarsely crushed chocolate sandwich cookies, divided

½ (16-ounce) container vanilla frosting

Preparation

1 Preheat oven to 350 degrees F. Coat a Bundt pan with cooking spray.

2 In a large bowl with an electric mixer, beat cake mix, eggs, water, oil, and chocolate syrup until thoroughly combined. Pour batter into pan.

3 Bake 35 to 40 minutes, or until toothpick comes out clean. Let cool 10 minutes, then invert onto a wire rack to cool completely. Cut cake in half horizontally and place bottom half on a serving platter.

4 In a large bowl with an electric mixer, beat butter, cream cheese, and vanilla until creamy. Add confectioners' sugar and heavy cream and beat until fluffy. Stir in ½ cup cookie crumbs. Spread filling evenly over bottom half of cake. Place top of cake over filling.

5 Place frosting in a microwave-safe bowl. Microwave 10 to 15 seconds, or until pourable, stirring as needed. Pour slowly over cake and sprinkle with remaining ½ cup cookie crumbs, pressing them gently onto frosting, so they don't fall off. Keep refrigerated.

Roasted Banana Bread Cake

You're probably familiar with the fact that the best banana bread is made from very ripe bananas. Well, that's good to know, but what do you do if you're ready to make one and your bananas aren't ripe enough? You roast them! As a matter of fact, we think that roasting the bananas, like we do in this recipe, makes this cake doubly delicious.

Serves 12

Ingredients

1 package yellow cake mix

1 (4-serving size) package instant banana pudding mix

3 eggs

1 cup water

⅓ cup vegetable oil

2 bananas, roasted and mashed (see Tip)

1 (16-ounce) container chocolate frosting

2 tablespoons chopped walnuts

Preparation

1 Preheat oven to 350 degrees F. Coat a Bundt pan with cooking spray.

2 In a large bowl, with an electric mixer, beat cake mix, pudding mix, eggs, water, and oil until blended. Add bananas and beat until thoroughly combined. Pour batter into pan.

3 Bake 40 to 45 minutes, or until toothpick comes out clean. Let cool 10 minutes, then invert onto a wire rack to cool completely. Place on platter.

4 Remove lid and foil cover from frosting container and place in microwave. Heat 20 to 30 seconds, or until pourable, stirring as needed. (Do not over-microwave.) Pour frosting evenly over cake and sprinkle with nuts.

Test Kitchen Tip: *To bring out the natural sugars in the bananas, roast them by placing them (with the skin on) on a baking sheet in a preheated 350-degree oven. Roast them 10 to 15 minutes, or until bananas are black on the outside. Then, cut skins open, remove bananas, and use as directed above.*

Pineapple Upside-Down Ring

The concept of baking a cake upside down dates back centuries ago when cakes were often baked in cast iron skillets over an open fire. It was a common practice for cooks to add fruit and sugar to the pan before the batter. This way, after it baked and the cake was flipped over, all the sugary goodness of the fruit would flavor the cake. And after all these years, that same philosophy still holds true.

Serves 12

Ingredients

2 tablespoons butter, melted

½ cup packed light brown sugar

6 pineapple slices (from a 20-ounce can) drained, with juice reserved

6 maraschino cherries

1 package yellow cake mix

Water (enough added to reserved pineapple juice to make 1 cup liquid)

⅓ cup vegetable oil

3 eggs

Preparation

1 Preheat oven to 350 degrees F. Coat a Bundt pan with cooking spray. Pour butter evenly over bottom of pan and sprinkle brown sugar evenly over butter. Arrange pineapple slices in a single layer over brown sugar and place a cherry in center of each slice.

2 In a large bowl with an electric mixer, beat cake mix, pineapple juice combined with enough water to make 1 cup liquid, the oil, and eggs until thoroughly combined. Pour batter into pan.

3 Bake 35 to 40 minutes, or until a toothpick comes out clean. Let cool 10 minutes, then invert cake onto a platter. Serve warm, or allow to cool completely before serving.

Test Kitchen Tip: *Since you must love pineapple or you wouldn't be making this cake, today is your lucky day! You'll have a few extra pineapple slices left over from the can, which you can nibble on while you're waiting for the cake to come out of the oven.*

Caribbean Rum Ring

If you're looking for a dessert that can turn a plain old evening into an island getaway, then this is it. With each forkful, you can almost feel the surf against your toes and hear the rhythm of the calypso music. This is one tropical vacation you won't need your passport for.

Serves 12

Ingredients

1 cup chopped pecans

1 package yellow cake mix

1 (4-serving size) package instant vanilla pudding mix

4 eggs

½ cup water

½ cup vegetable oil

½ cup rum

SAUCE

1 stick (½ cup) butter

1 cup sugar

¼ cup rum

¼ cup water

Preparation

1   Preheat oven to 325 degrees F. Coat a Bundt pan with cooking spray. Sprinkle pecans evenly over bottom of pan.

2   In a large bowl with an electric mixer, beat cake mix, pudding mix, eggs, the ½ cup water, oil, and the ½ cup rum until thoroughly combined. Pour batter into pan.

3   Bake 45 to 50 minutes, or until a toothpick comes out clean. Using a fork, prick holes in cake while it's warm and still in pan; set aside.

4   Meanwhile, in a saucepan, combine sauce ingredients; bring to a boil. Reduce heat to low and simmer 5 minutes, stirring occasionally. Do not allow to boil over.

5   Slowly pour sauce evenly over warm cake in pan. Let stand 1 hour, or until cool. Invert cake onto a platter and serve.

Did You Know? *Pricking the cake with a fork allows the sauce to soak into all of the cake, so that every bite is packed with goodness.*

Royal Pumpkin Spice Cake

Adding canned pumpkin to a cake mix is like witnessing Cinderella's Fairy Godmother turn a pumpkin into a stagecoach to take her to the ball. What it does is magically transform a simple dessert into one that's fit for a king or, in this case, a prince - a very charming prince. Consider the spoon your magic wand and let's get started!

Serves 12

Ingredients

1 package spice cake mix, divided

1 cup cinnamon baking chips

1 cup canned pumpkin (not pumpkin pie mix)

½ cup water

⅓ cup vegetable oil

4 eggs

¼ cup confectioners' sugar

½ teaspoon ground cinnamon

Preparation

1 Preheat oven to 325 degrees F. Coat a Bundt pan with cooking spray. In a small bowl, toss 2 teaspoons cake mix with baking chips until evenly coated; set aside. (See note.)

2 In a large bowl with an electric mixer, beat remaining cake mix, pumpkin, water, oil, and eggs until thoroughly combined. Stir baking chips into batter, then pour into pan.

3 Bake 35 to 40 minutes, or until toothpick comes out clean. Cool 15 minutes, then invert onto a wire rack to cool completely.

4 In a small bowl, combine confectioners' sugar and cinnamon. Sprinkle over cake and serve.

Did You Know? *Tossing the baking chips in a little dry cake mix before adding them to the batter will prevent them from falling to the bottom of the pan while baking. Pretty magical, huh?*

HOLIDAY SPECIA

Party-Hearty Margarita Cake

If you're flipping through this book in search of that "special cake" to bring to this summer's potluck or you're just looking for a dessert that'll help cure those mid-winter blues, then you've landed on the right page! This cake has all the taste and excitement of a fresh and fruity margarita teamed up with the yumminess of a super moist cake.

Serves 12

Ingredients

1 package white cake mix

1 cup strawberry margarita mix

⅓ cup vegetable oil

3 eggs

FROSTING

2 sticks (1 cup) butter, softened

4 cups confectioners' sugar

2 tablespoons strawberry margarita mix

2 teaspoons lime juice

Preparation

1 Preheat oven to 350 degrees F. Coat a Bundt pan with cooking spray.

2 In a large bowl with an electric mixer, beat cake mix, 1 cup margarita mix, the oil, and eggs until thoroughly combined. Pour batter into pan.

3 Bake 35 to 40 minutes, or until a toothpick comes out clean. Let cool completely, then invert onto a platter.

4 Meanwhile, in a large bowl with an electric mixer, beat frosting ingredients until smooth; frost cake. Keep refrigerated.

Fancy It Up: For that extra-special touch, garnish with fresh strawberries and lime slices, along with a sprinkle of colored sugar.

Cinnamon Roll Breakfast Ring

The trick to getting everyone to rise 'n' shine in the morning is right here on this page. Even your late-morning risers are going to skip hitting the snooze button and rush into the kitchen for a slice of this sweet treat, with a big glass of milk or a steaming cup of coffee. It doesn't matter whether they're in it for the gooey frosting or the cinnamon swirl, it's just nice to have them back around the table!

Serves 12

Ingredients

1 cup finely chopped pecans

2 tablespoons light brown sugar

2 teaspoons ground cinnamon

1 package yellow cake mix, divided

4 eggs

1 cup sour cream

⅓ cup vegetable oil

¼ cup water

2 teaspoons vanilla extract

FROSTING

3 ounces cream cheese, softened

2 tablespoons butter

1 tablespoon milk

1 cup confectioners' sugar

Preparation

1 Preheat oven to 350 degrees F. Coat a Bundt pan with cooking spray.

2 In a small bowl, combine pecans, brown sugar, cinnamon, and 2 tablespoons cake mix; mix well. Sprinkle ¼ of pecan mixture in bottom of pan; reserving remaining mixture.

3 In a large bowl with an electric mixer, beat remaining cake mix, the eggs, sour cream, oil, water, and vanilla until thoroughly combined. Pour half the batter over pecan mixture in the pan. Sprinkle remaining pecan mixture over batter, then pour remaining batter on top.

4 Bake 40 to 45 minutes, or until toothpick comes out clean. Let cool 10 minutes, then invert onto a wire rack to cool completely.

5 In a medium bowl with an electric mixer, beat frosting ingredients until smooth. Frost top of cake. Keep refrigerated.

Skinny Sunshine Berry Cake

When you're craving big flavor, without a side of guilt, then this is the cake you've got to make. With only 193 calories and 28 grams of carbs per slice, this Bundt cake delivers a guilt-free taste of decadence. Now, doesn't that make your day feel a whole lot sunnier?

Serves 16

Ingredients

1 package sugar-free yellow cake mix

2 (4-serving size) packages instant sugar-free lemon pudding mix

1 cup fat-free evaporated milk

½ cup canola oil

½ cup water

1 teaspoon lemon extract

1 cup liquid egg substitute

1 (8-ounce) container sugar-free frozen whipped topping, thawed, divided

1-½ cups sliced strawberries, plus extra for garnish

Preparation

1 Preheat oven to 350 degrees F. Coat a Bundt pan with cooking spray.

2 In a large bowl with an electric mixer, beat cake mix, pudding mix, evaporated milk, oil, water, and lemon extract until smooth. Beat in egg substitute until thoroughly combined, then pour into pan.

3 Bake 40 to 45 minutes, or until a toothpick comes out clean. Let cool 15 minutes, then invert onto a wire rack to cool completely.

4 Place cake on a platter and cut in half horizontally. Gently remove top and set aside. Spread 2 cups whipped topping over bottom half of cake. Top with 1-½ cups sliced strawberries. Replace top half of cake. Dollop remaining whipped topping on top of cake and garnish with extra strawberries. Keep refrigerated.

Fancy It Up:. Feel free to garnish this with some thinly sliced lemon to make it extra-special. And if you prefer to make this with regular, instead of sugar-free ingredients, you totally can – it's up to you!

LIGHTER OPTION

Oktoberfest Beer Cake with Chocolate Glaze

We took some inspiration from Germany's Oktoberfest and came up with a cake that'll have everyone clinking their beer steins in celebration! The beer adds a rich, nutty flavor to an off-the-shelf boxed cake mix, making for an unbelievably easy and tasty combination. Top it off with a chocolate glaze and you're in for a real treat.

Serves 12

Ingredients

1 package fudge marble cake mix

½ cup sour cream

1 cup stout beer

¼ cup vegetable oil

3 eggs

GLAZE

1 cup confectioners' sugar

1 tablespoon cocoa powder

2 tablespoons stout beer

Preparation

1 Preheat oven to 350 degrees F. Coat a Bundt pan with cooking spray.

2 In a large bowl with an electric mixer, beat cake mix, sour cream, 1 cup beer, the oil, and eggs until thoroughly combined, then pour into pan.

3 Bake 35 to 40 minutes, or until toothpick comes out clean. Let cool 10 minutes, then invert onto a wire rack to cool completely.

4 In a small bowl, whisk glaze ingredients until smooth. Drizzle over cake and let sit until glaze hardens.

So Many Options: *Although we suggest making this with a stout beer, which is a darker beer with a bolder flavor, feel free to swap it out with your favorite or with whatever you have in the fridge.*

Pink Lemonade Stand Cake

When the kids in the neighborhood start opening up their lemonade stands for the summer, you know it's a good time to bake up this refreshing Bundt cake. It's got pink lemonade baked right into the batter, so you know every bite is going to be tangy, sweet, and oh-so-scrumptious. You might even think about going into business with them!

Serves 12

Ingredients

1 package lemon cake mix, divided

1 (4-serving size) package instant lemon pudding mix

½ cup water

⅓ cup vegetable oil

4 eggs

1 (12-ounce) can frozen pink lemonade concentrate, thawed, divided

1-½ cups confectioners' sugar

Preparation

1 Preheat oven to 350 degrees F. Coat a Bundt pan with cooking spray and lightly dust with 1 tablespoon cake mix.

2 In a large bowl with an electric mixer, beat remaining cake mix, pudding mix, water, oil, eggs, and ¾ cup pink lemonade concentrate until thoroughly combined. Pour batter into pan.

3 Bake 40 to 45 minutes, or until toothpick comes out clean. Let cool 15 minutes, then invert onto a wire rack to cool completely.

4 In a small bowl, whisk confectioners' sugar and ¼ cup pink lemonade concentrate until smooth. Drizzle over cake and serve.

Test Kitchen Tip: *There will be about a 1/2 cup of lemonade concentrate left over, which is just enough to whip up a small batch of icy cold pink lemonade, so you can sit back and relax before digging in. Hey, why not? You earned it!*

Candy Cane Christmas Ring

We hope you've bought an extra-large stocking this year, because once your gang gets a taste of this yummy peppermint cake, you're going to move up to the top of their list! Not only is this cake holiday festive on the outside, but inside there's a beautiful red and white swirl that makes it look like a candy cane. Serve this with a hot toddy and you just might earn yourself some bonus points.

Serves 12

Ingredients

1 package white cake mix

1 cup water

⅓ cup vegetable oil

2 teaspoons peppermint extract

3 eggs

2 teaspoons red food color

½ (16-ounce) container white frosting

Holiday red, white, and green nonpareils for garnish

Preparation

1 Preheat oven to 350 degrees F. Coat a Bundt pan with cooking spray.

2 In a large bowl with an electric mixer, beat cake mix, water, oil, peppermint extract, and eggs until thoroughly combined. Pour half the batter into a medium bowl and stir in food color until well blended.

3 Pour half the white batter evenly into Bundt pan. Slowly pour all of red batter over white batter. Pour remaining white batter on top.

4 Bake 35 to 40 minutes, or until toothpick comes out clean. Cool 10 minutes, then invert onto a wire rack to cool completely. Place cake on platter.

5 Place frosting in a microwave-safe bowl. Microwave 10 to 15 seconds, or until pourable, stirring as needed. Drizzle over cake, then sprinkle with nonpareils. Let frosting harden before serving.

So Many Options: *For an extra candy cane taste and look, feel free to swap out the nonpareils for crushed candy cane bits.*

HOLIDAY SPECIAL

Season's Greetings Holiday Fruitcake

You know Christmas is around the corner when your grocery store starts setting out the fruitcake. It used to be that fruitcake was one of the most loved cakes of the season, but nowadays the store-bought kind is dry and boring. All the more reason to make it homemade! You won't want to pass on (or re-gift!) this fruitcake, since ours is super-moist and studded with lots of dried fruit, nuts, and yummy apricot nectar.

Serves 12

Ingredients

1 package spice cake mix

1 (4-serving size) package instant vanilla pudding mix

1 cup apricot nectar

½ cup vegetable oil

4 eggs

1 (16-ounce) container mixed candied fruit

1 cup raisins

1 cup chopped pecans

Preparation

1 Preheat oven to 350 degrees F. Coat a Bundt pan with cooking spray.

2 In a large bowl with an electric mixer, beat cake mix, pudding mix, apricot nectar, oil, and eggs until thoroughly combined. Stir in candied fruit, raisins, and pecans, then pour into pan.

3 Bake 55 to 60 minutes, or until a toothpick comes out clean. Let cool 10 minutes, then invert onto a wire rack to cool completely.

HOLIDAY SPECIAL

Lots of Layers

Tall, Dark, & Handsome Chocolate Cake

When we first created this chocolaty cake for our TV segment, we knew it needed an irresistible name to go with it. We took a step back, realized what a great looking cake we had made, and came to a unanimous decision. So, it's our pleasure to introduce you to a cake that's as tasty as it is "tall, dark, & handsome." We promise it'll melt your heart.

Serves 12

Ingredients

1 package chocolate cake mix

1 cup brewed coffee

⅓ cup vegetable oil

3 eggs

2 (16-ounce) containers chocolate frosting

4 tablespoons caramel topping

8 chocolate-covered caramel candies, chopped (We tested this with Rolos®.)

Preparation

1 Preheat oven to 350 degrees F. Coat the bottom of 2 (8-inch) round cake pans with cooking spray.

2 In a large bowl with an electric mixer, beat cake mix, coffee, oil, and eggs until thoroughly combined. Pour batter evenly into cake pans. Bake 25 to 30 minutes, or until a toothpick inserted in center comes out clean. Let cool 10 minutes, then remove to wire racks to cool completely.

3 Cut each cake in half horizontally to make 4 layers. Place 1 layer on a platter and spread half a container of frosting on top. Drizzle 1 tablespoon caramel topping over frosting. Repeat with remaining cake layers and finish with frosting. Drizzle with caramel topping and garnish with chopped candies.

Outrageous Orange Juice Cake

If the only way you've ever had orange juice is out of a glass with breakfast, then you're in for a real treat. This cake has a "fresh-squeezed" taste that's outrageously good. And when it's topped with our rich, homemade cream cheese frosting, you can bet there'll be smiles all around.

Serves 10

Ingredients

1 package yellow cake mix

1 (4-serving size) package orange-flavored gelatin mix

1 cup orange juice with pulp

¾ cup vegetable oil

3 eggs

1 (15-ounce) can mandarin oranges, drained, for garnish

1 bunch fresh mint

FROSTING

½ stick (¼ cup) butter, softened

1 (8-ounce) package cream cheese, softened

1 teaspoon vanilla extract

6 cups confectioners' sugar

Preparation

1 Preheat oven to 350 degrees F. Coat the bottom of 2 (9-inch) round cake pans with cooking spray.

2 In a large bowl with an electric mixer, beat cake mix, gelatin mix, orange juice, oil, and eggs until thoroughly combined. Pour batter evenly into cake pans. Bake 25 to 30 minutes, or until a toothpick inserted in center comes out clean. Let cool 10 minutes, then remove to wire racks to cool completely.

3 To make frosting, in a large bowl with an electric mixer, beat butter, cream cheese, and vanilla until creamy. Slowly add confectioners' sugar, beating until smooth.

4 Place one cake layer on a serving platter and frost top. Place second layer on top and frost top and sides of cake. Garnish with mandarin oranges and mint. Keep refrigerated.

All-Occasion Layer Cake

It's always a good idea to have a foolproof cake recipe that works for any occasion, whether it be a family get-together, church potluck, or a simple mid-afternoon snack. It has to be something that's easy to make, but that tastes extra-special...wait a minute, we just described this cake! By adding some white chocolate into the batter and frosting it with a from-scratch chocolate buttercream, this cake is crazy-good and great for all occasions!

Serves 8

Ingredients

1 package white cake mix

1-¼ cups water

⅓ cup vegetable oil

3 eggs

1 teaspoon vanilla extract

1 (4-ounce) package white chocolate baking bar, finely chopped

FROSTING

1-½ sticks (¾ cup) butter, softened

1 teaspoon vanilla extract

½ cup unsweetened cocoa powder

5 tablespoons milk

6 cups confectioners' sugar

Preparation

1 Preheat oven to 350 degrees F. Coat the bottom of 2 (8-inch) round cake pans with cooking spray.

2 In a large bowl with an electric mixer, beat cake mix, water, oil, eggs, and 1 teaspoon vanilla until thoroughly combined; stir in white chocolate. Pour batter evenly into pans. Bake 25 to 30 minutes, or until a toothpick inserted in center comes out clean. Let cool 10 minutes, then remove to wire racks to cool completely.

3 To make frosting, in a large bowl with an electric mixer, beat butter and 1 teaspoon vanilla until creamy. Add cocoa and milk, beating until thoroughly combined. Slowly add confectioners' sugar, beating until smooth.

4 Place one cake layer on a platter and frost top. Place second layer on top and frost top and sides of cake. Keep refrigerated.

Test Kitchen Tip: *You can make your cake look even more homemade just by adding a swirl pattern to the frosting! To do this you will need to frost your cake, then using the back of a soup spoon, lightly make a quarter of a turn in the frosting and lift it up. This will create a swirl with a peak.*

Spring Bouquet Coconut Cake

This cake is a perfect example of how something so simple can be so beautiful. The coconut milk adds a touch of richness, the buttercream frosting simply melts in your mouth, and the bouquet of edible flowers gives it a springtime feel. This proves that anyone can have a "green thumb" in the kitchen!

Serves 8

Ingredients

1 package white cake mix

1 cup coconut milk
(not cream of coconut)

⅓ cup vegetable oil

3 eggs

2 cups flaked coconut

FROSTING

2 sticks (1 cup) butter

¼ cup heavy cream

1 teaspoon vanilla extract

6 cups confectioners' sugar

¼ cup gum drops,
cut into quarters

Preparation

1 Preheat oven to 350 degrees F. Coat the bottom of 2 (8-inch) round cake pans with cooking spray.

2 In a large bowl with an electric mixer, beat cake mix, coconut milk, oil, and eggs; mix until thoroughly combined. Pour batter evenly into cake pans. Bake 25 to 30 minutes, or until a toothpick inserted in center comes out clean. Let cool 10 minutes, then remove to wire racks to cool completely.

3 To make frosting, in a large bowl with an electric mixer, beat butter, heavy cream, and vanilla until creamy. Slowly add confectioners' sugar, beating until smooth.

4 To make filling, place 1 cup frosting in a separate bowl and stir in quartered gum drops. Place 1 cake layer on a serving platter and spread evenly with gum drop filling.

5 Place second cake layer on top and frost top and sides of cake with remaining frosting. Sprinkle coconut over entire cake. Keep refrigerated.

Fancy It Up: *To make our colorful and edible flower bouquet, all you've got to do is sprinkle a cutting board with a bit of granulated sugar. Then, using a rolling pin, roll out 6 to 7 gum drops, one at a time, until each is about 1/8-inch thick and 2-inches around. Gently fold and roll each gum drop to create a flower. Cut out "leaves" using green gum drops that have been rolled out, and arrange as shown.*

Patty's Green Pistachio Pudding Cake

Growing up, Patty loved when her mom would serve her a big slice of "green cake" for dessert. It was one of her favorites, and one that many of us have grown up with, too. While this cake isn't new, we did update it to make it even creamier and more moist than ever. You're going to love how much of the pistachio flavor comes through in each bite!

Serves 8

Ingredients

1 package white cake mix, divided

2 (4-serving size) packages instant pistachio pudding mix

½ cup milk

½ cup vegetable oil

½ cup water

5 eggs

FROSTING

1 cup (½ pint) heavy cream

1 cup milk

1 (4-serving size) package instant pistachio pudding mix

Preparation

1 Preheat oven to 350 degrees F. Coat the bottom of 2 (8-inch) round cake pans with cooking spray, then lightly dust with 1 tablespoon cake mix.

2 In a large bowl with an electric mixer, beat remaining cake mix, 2 packages pudding mix, ½ cup milk, the oil, and water until thoroughly combined. Beat in eggs until well mixed. Pour batter evenly into cake pans.

3 Bake 25 to 30 minutes, or until a toothpick inserted in center comes out clean. Cool 15 minutes, then remove to wire racks to cool completely.

4 To make frosting, in a medium bowl with an electric mixer, beat heavy cream with 1 cup milk and 1 package pudding mix until thickened. Place 1 cake layer upside down on a serving plate and frost the top. Place second layer over first and frost top and sides of cake. Keep refrigerated.

Fancy It Up: To give this a bakery-fancy touch, decorate the bottom edge of the cake with chopped pistachio nuts. Oh, and if you have some left over, sprinkle those on top!

Candy Dish Layered Cake

A wise man once said, "9 out of 10 people love chocolate. The 10th person always lies." Now, we may not be able to confirm that, but we do know that if you put out this cake at your next get-together, everyone is going to want some. Not only is it topped with an assortment of their favorite candy, but beneath it all is a super moist layer cake surrounded by chocolate candy bars!

Serves 12

Ingredients

1 package yellow cake mix

1 (4-serving size) package instant vanilla pudding mix

1 cup milk

⅓ cup vegetable oil

3 eggs

1 (16-ounce) can chocolate frosting

15 (1.5-ounce) crisp wafer candy bars (We used KitKat®.)

1 chocolate truffle

2 cups candy-coated chocolate peanut candies

2 cups small nonpareil candies

2 cups chocolate-covered almonds

Ribbon for decoration (optional)

Preparation

1 Preheat oven to 350 degrees F. Coat the bottom of 2 (8-inch) round cake pans with cooking spray.

2 In a large bowl with an electric mixer, beat cake mix, pudding mix, milk, oil, and eggs until thoroughly combined. Pour batter evenly into cake pans. Bake 25 to 30 minutes, or until a toothpick inserted in center comes out clean. Cool 15 minutes, then remove to wire racks to cool completely.

3 Place 1 cake layer on a platter, and frost top. Place second layer on top and frost top and sides of cake. Arrange candy bars around the cake, as shown, pressing them gently to secure. The candy bars should extend higher than the cake.

4 Place chocolate truffle in center of cake. Arrange 6 more candy bars on top of cake, as shown. Fill each wedge with remaining candies, as shown. Tie a ribbon around the cake, if desired.

So Many Options! *You can change your candy selection to fit the season, a holiday, or your special occasion. For example, for a spooky Halloween look, top your cake with gummy worms, chocolate spiders, and orange and black-colored candies.*

Toasted Almond Crunch Cake

We could tell you that you should make this cake because almonds are incredibly nutritious and are a good source of healthy fats, fiber, protein, and vitamins E & B. But, to be honest, we feel that the best reason to make this cake is simply because there's lots of rich almond taste woven into every forkful. From the sponge-like cake to the crunchy almond topping, this cake is nutty-delicious!

Serves 10

Ingredients

1 package yellow cake mix

1 cup almond milk

3 eggs

⅓ cup vegetable oil

1 teaspoon almond extract

1-½ cups toasted sliced almonds for garnish (see Tip)

FROSTING

1 stick (½ cup) butter, softened

1 teaspoon vanilla extract

5 cups confectioners' sugar

5 tablespoons milk

Preparation

1 Preheat oven to 350 degrees F. Coat the bottom of 2 (9-inch) round cake pans with cooking spray.

2 In a large bowl with an electric mixer, beat cake mix, almond milk, eggs, oil, and almond extract until thoroughly combined. Pour evenly into baking pans. Bake 20 to 25 minutes, or until a toothpick inserted in center comes out clean. Let cool 10 minutes, then remove to wire racks to cool completely.

3 To make frosting, in a large bowl with an electric mixer, beat butter and vanilla until creamy. Slowly add confectioners' sugar and milk, beating until smooth.

4 Place one cake layer on a platter and frost top. Place second layer on top and frost top and sides of cake. Sprinkle almonds evenly on top and sides of cake, pressing gently to secure. Keep refrigerated.

Test Kitchen Tip: *The best way to toast almonds is to place them in a single layer on a rimmed baking sheet in a 350 degree oven for 3 to 4 minutes, or until golden. Check often.*

Hoppy Easter Bunny Cake

Just wait until your gang gets a "peep" (or is it "peek"?) at this fun and colorful Easter dessert. They're not going to stop raving about it! And don't think for a minute that this is one of those cakes that's just pretty to look at, since each forkful is truly a delight. We do have one suggestion though...keep it out of sight until it's time for dessert or your bunnies may "magically" disappear.

Serves 11 (2 bunnies each)

Ingredients

1 package white cake mix

1 cup water

⅓ cup vegetable oil

3 eggs

1-½ teaspoons vanilla extract

3 to 4 drops neon blue food color

1 (16-ounce) can vanilla frosting

1 cup flaked coconut

2 to 3 drops green food color

22 marshmallow bunnies, assorted colors

About 50 jelly beans

Preparation

1 Preheat oven to 350 degrees F. Coat the bottom of 2 (8-inch) round cake pans with cooking spray.

2 In a large bowl with an electric mixer, beat cake mix, water, oil, eggs, and vanilla until thoroughly combined. Place ½ cup batter in a small bowl; stir in blue food color until evenly blended and set aside. Pour remaining batter evenly into cake pans. Place spoonfuls of blue batter randomly over batter in cake pans and swirl with a butter knife.

3 Bake 25 to 30 minutes, or until a toothpick inserted in center comes out clean. Let cool 10 minutes, then remove to wire racks to cool completely.

4 Place 1 cake layer on a serving platter and frost top. Place second layer over first and frost top and sides of cake.

5 In a small bowl, combine coconut and green food color; mix until thoroughly blended. Sprinkle coconut evenly over top of cake. Place marshmallow bunnies around sides of cake, alternating colors and pressing them gently to secure. Decorate top edge with jelly beans, as shown.

"Wicked Easy" Boston Cream Pie

When Bostonians want to emphasize how good or bad something is they use the word "wicked." So, for example, if you served them a slice of this classic cake you'd hear, "This is wicked good!" And if you were nice enough to share the recipe they'd say, "It's wicked easy, too!" Hey, what can we say, we like making the classics deliciously easy.

Serves 10

Ingredients

1 package yellow cake mix

½ cup sour cream

1 cup water

⅓ cup vegetable oil

3 eggs

1-½ teaspoons vanilla extract

1 (4-serving size) package instant vanilla pudding mix

1 cup cold milk

1 cup dark chocolate chips

¾ cup heavy cream

Preparation

1 Preheat oven to 350 degrees F. Coat the bottom of 2 (8-inch) round cake pans with cooking spray.

2 In a large bowl with an electric mixer, beat cake mix, sour cream, water, oil, eggs, and vanilla until thoroughly combined. Pour batter evenly into cake pans. Bake 25 to 30 minutes, or until a toothpick inserted in center comes out clean. Let cool 10 minutes, then invert onto wire racks to cool completely.

3 In a medium bowl, whisk pudding mix and milk until mixture thickens. Place one cake layer on a platter and spread pudding mixture over top. Place second cake layer over pudding.

4 In a medium bowl, place chocolate chips; set aside. In a small saucepan over medium heat, heat heavy cream until hot, but not boiling. Pour heavy cream over chocolate chips and stir until chips are melted and smooth. Let cool 5 to 10 minutes, or until slightly thickened. Spoon chocolate over top of cake and spread evenly, letting some of the chocolate drip down sides. Keep refrigerated.

Did You Know? *As you may have guessed by now, a Boston Cream Pie isn't really a pie at all - it's a cake! No one is 100% sure why there's a mismatch, but it's likely because when this dessert was first created, it was baked in a more traditional pie tin versus a cake pan.*

Simple Southern Hummingbird Cake

We can't tell you whether this cake got its name from being so sweet that it attracts hummingbirds or being so good that it causes people to hum after just a taste. What we can tell you is that Hummingbird Cake has been a popular Southern dessert since the 1970s and a popular island dessert before that. It's a cake that's stood the test of time because it features the perfect combination of tropical fruit flavors.

Serves 12

Ingredients

1 package yellow cake mix

1 (4-serving size) package instant vanilla pudding mix

½ cup vegetable oil

¾ cup water

4 eggs

1 ripe banana, mashed

1 teaspoon ground cinnamon

1 (8-ounce) package cream cheese, softened

½ cup confectioners' sugar

1 (16-ounce) container frozen whipped topping, thawed

½ cup red maraschino cherries, well drained, chopped

1 (8-ounce) can crushed pineapple, well drained

1 cup chopped pecans

Preparation

1　Preheat oven to 350 degrees F. Coat the bottom of 2 (8-inch) round cake pans with cooking spray.

2　In a large bowl with an electric mixer, beat cake mix, pudding mix, oil, water, eggs, banana, and cinnamon until thoroughly combined. Pour batter evenly into baking pans. Bake 35 to 40 minutes, or until a toothpick inserted in center comes out clean. Let cool 10 minutes, then remove to wire racks to cool completely.

3　In a large bowl with an electric mixer, beat cream cheese and confectioners' sugar until smooth. Fold in whipped topping. Place ½ the mixture in another bowl, then stir in cherries, pineapple, and pecans.

4　Place first cake layer on a platter and spread half the fruit mixture on top. Place second cake layer on top and spread top with remaining fruit mixture. Frost sides of cake with plain cream cheese mixture. Keep refrigerated.

Fancy It Up: *To make this look picture-perfect, just garnish the top with cherries and the bottom edge with additional chopped pecans.*

Secret Ingredient Double Chocolate Cake

The picture says it all. This cake is so decadent-looking that it's nearly impossible to resist sneaking a finger full of our extra fudgy frosting. And if you thought that was all, just wait until you serve yourself a slice. We've added a special ingredient to the batter that makes it melt-in-your-mouth good — it's mayonnaise. Trust us on this one, you're going to love it.

Serves 10

Ingredients

1 package dark chocolate cake mix

3 eggs

1 cup water

½ cup mayonnaise

1 tablespoon dark cocoa powder

FROSTING

1-½ sticks (¾ cup) butter, softened

½ cup dark cocoa powder

2 teaspoons vanilla extract

5 cups confectioners' sugar

⅓ cup plus 1 tablespoon milk

Preparation

1 Preheat oven to 350 degrees F. Coat the bottom of 2 (9-inch) round cake pans with cooking spray.

2 In a large bowl with an electric mixer, beat cake mix, eggs, water, mayonnaise, and 1 tablespoon cocoa powder until thoroughly combined. Pour batter evenly into cake pans. Bake 20 to 25 minutes, or until a toothpick inserted in center comes out clean. Let cool 10 minutes, then remove to wire racks to cool completely.

3 To make frosting, in a large bowl with an electric mixer, beat butter, ½ cup cocoa powder, and vanilla until creamy. Slowly add confectioners' sugar and milk, beating until smooth.

4 Place 1 cake layer upside-down on a platter and frost top. Place second layer on top and frost top and sides. Keep refrigerated.

Test Kitchen Tip: *The trick to getting a super dark chocolate taste and look is to make sure you use dark cocoa powder. You can find it in the same area as all the other baking supplies in your market.*

Holly Jolly Santa Cake

Add a little whimsy to your Christmas dessert spread with this easy and inspiring holiday cake. They'll marvel at your snowmen, all dressed up to look like Santa, but the real "ho ho ho's" will come once they get a taste of the moist cake and fluffy cream cheese frosting. We hope you're ready to have yourself an extra-special, holly jolly Christmas!

Serves 12

Ingredients

1 package white cake mix

½ cup sour cream

1 cup water

¼ cup vegetable oil

3 egg whites

3 teaspoons red food color

12 large strawberries, stems removed

I tube black piping gel

Silver decorating sugar (optional)

FROSTING

2 (8-ounce) packages cream cheese, softened

3 cups confectioners' sugar

1 (16-ounce) container frozen whipped topping, thawed

Preparation

1 Preheat oven to 350 degrees F. Coat bottom of 2 (8-inch) round cake pans with cooking spray.

2 In a large bowl with an electric mixer, beat cake mix, sour cream, water, oil, and egg whites until combined. Place half the batter in a separate bowl and stir in food color until combined. Pour red batter into one pan and white batter into second pan. Bake 25 to 30 minutes, or until toothpick comes out clean. Cool 10 minutes, then remove to wire racks to cool completely. Cut cakes in half horizontally, making 4 layers.

3 To make frosting, in a large bowl with an electric mixer, beat cream cheese and confectioners' sugar until smooth. Fold in whipped topping until combined, reserving ½ cup for decorating. Place one white cake layer on platter and frost top. Add a red layer and frost top; repeat with remaining layers and frosting. Frost top and sides of cake.

4 Cut off tip of each strawberry and, using a plastic storage bag with the corner cut, pipe about 1 tablespoon of frosting between pieces of each strawberry. Decorate using remaining frosting and piping gel. Sprinkle cake with decorating sugar, if desired, and add snowmen.

HOLIDAY SPECIAL

Birthday Surprise Piñata Cake

Imagine the look on the birthday boy or girl's face when they cut into their cake and discover yet another birthday surprise - their favorite candy! Our inspiration for this cake comes from the childhood tradition of smashing a colorful piñata stuffed full of treats. However, rather than smashing ours with a stick, we recommend cutting it with a knife before digging in. Don't be surprised if this becomes your most requested birthday cake!

Serves 12

Ingredients

1 package devil's food cake mix

1 (4-serving size) package instant chocolate pudding mix

1 cup water

⅓ cup vegetable oil

3 eggs

2 cups candy-coated chocolates for filling

FROSTING

1-½ sticks (¾ cup) butter, softened

3 ounces unsweetened chocolate baking bar, melted

2 teaspoons vanilla extract

6 cups confectioners' sugar

5 tablespoons milk

Preparation

1 Preheat oven to 350 degrees F. Coat the bottom of 2 (8-inch) round cake pans with cooking spray.

2 In a large bowl with an electric mixer, beat cake mix, pudding mix, water, oil, and eggs until thoroughly combined. Pour batter evenly into cake pans. Bake 25 to 30 minutes, or until a toothpick inserted in center comes out clean. Let cool 10 minutes, then invert onto wire racks to cool completely.

3 To make frosting, in a large bowl with an electric mixer, beat butter, chocolate, and vanilla until creamy. Slowly add in confectioners' sugar and milk and beat until smooth.

4 Cut each cake in half horizontally to make 4 layers. Cut a 3-inch hole in the center of 2 of the cake layers, using a 3-inch bowl as a guide. Place 1 uncut cake layer on a platter and frost top. Place 1 cut layer on top and frost. Place second cut layer on top and frost. Fill hole with candy. Place remaining uncut cake layer on top and frost top and sides. Keep refrigerated.

6-Layer Carrot Cake Stack

Go ahead and count them — three layers of super moist carrot cake and three layers of smooth-as-can-be cream cheese frosting. If the photo has you too distracted to do the math, we'll help you out - that's six total layers of absolute deliciousness. Oh, and for our carrot cake lovers (you know who you are), we hope you're ready to say your goodbyes to that old recipe you used to love, because this one is about to take its place.

Serves 10

Ingredients

1 package carrot cake mix

1 cup buttermilk

½ cup vegetable oil

¼ cup water

3 eggs

½ cup shredded carrots

1 tablespoon confectioners' sugar

2 tablespoons chopped walnuts

FROSTING

1 (8-ounce) package cream cheese, softened

½ stick (¼ cup) butter, softened

1 teaspoon vanilla extract

3 cups confectioners' sugar

Preparation

1 Preheat oven to 350 degrees F. Coat a 10- x 15-inch rimmed baking sheet with cooking spray.

2 In a large bowl with an electric mixer, beat cake mix, buttermilk, oil, water, and eggs until thoroughly combined. Stir in carrots. Pour batter evenly onto baking sheet. Bake 15 to 20 minutes, or until a toothpick inserted in center comes out clean; let cool 10 minutes. Sprinkle a cutting board with 1 tablespoon confectioners' sugar. Run a knife around edge of baking sheet. Invert cake onto cutting board to finish cooling.

3 To make frosting, in a large bowl with an electric mixer, beat cream cheese, butter, and vanilla until creamy. Slowly add in 3 cups confectioners' sugar, and beat until smooth.

4 Cut cake crosswise into 3 equal pieces, each measuring 5- x 10-inches. Spread filling evenly onto each piece of cake. Place 1 cake layer onto a platter, then stack remaining layers on top. Garnish with walnuts.

Finishing Touch: *To give this its signature fresh look, garnish with some additional grated carrot and chopped nuts. After all, we eat with our eyes!*

3-Ingredient Banana Pyramid

You won't find anyone hitching a camel to visit this pyramid, but you can bet there'll be a line at your kitchen counter for a look and a taste of what is one of our favorite summertime desserts. We like it because it looks a little out of the ordinary, but it's made from a classic and well-loved combo of chocolate, bananas, and whipped topping.

Serves 10

Ingredients

1 package chocolate cake mix, batter prepared according to package directions

1 (16-ounce) container frozen whipped topping, thawed, divided

3 large bananas, peeled

Preparation

1 Preheat oven to 350 degrees F. Coat a 10- x 15-inch rimmed baking sheet with cooking spray and line with wax paper. Pour cake batter evenly onto baking sheet.

2 Bake 22 to 24 minutes, or until a toothpick inserted in center comes out clean. Allow to cool completely, then invert onto a cutting board. Remove wax paper. Trim 1/8-inch off edges all around cake, setting aside for garnish. Cut crosswise into 3 equal pieces, each measuring 5- x 10-inches. Leave pieces in place.

3 Reserve 1 cup whipped topping to frost cake; set aside. Spread some of the remaining whipped topping over middle piece of cake, completely covering it. Place 2 bananas next to each other over whipped topping, then top with more whipped topping. Place third banana over that and cover with remaining whipped topping. (See photo)

4 Bring up 2 side pieces of cake to form a triangle. Transfer to a serving platter and frost cake with reserved whipped topping. Grate or crumble cake trimmings to garnish. Refrigerate at least 1 hour before slicing and serving. Keep refrigerated.

Yuletide Log Cake

The burning of the Yule log is a Christmas tradition that dates back hundreds of years. Somewhere along the way, folks became inspired to start baking cakes that resembled the symbolic log. Nowadays, you can find this beautiful dessert in practically every bakery come Christmastime. Luckily for you, we've come up with an easy way to make this bakery-fancy dessert, so you can make your own Christmas traditions come to life.

Serves 10

Ingredients

6 eggs

1 package yellow cake mix

½ cup water

¼ cup vegetable oil

1 tablespoon all-purpose flour

FROSTING

6 tablespoons butter

¾ cup unsweetened cocoa powder

1-½ teaspoons vanilla extract

5 cups confectioners' sugar

⅓ cup milk

Preparation

1 Preheat oven to 350 degrees F. Coat a 10- x 15-inch rimmed baking sheet with cooking spray. Line with wax paper, then coat with cooking spray.

2 In a large bowl with an electric mixer, beat eggs 1 to 2 minutes, or until thickened. Add cake mix, water, and oil and beat until thoroughly combined. Pour 3-½ cups batter evenly onto baking sheet. (Prepare remaining batter according to Tip.) Bake 10 to 12 minutes, or until a toothpick inserted comes out clean.

3 Sprinkle a kitchen towel with flour and invert cake onto towel; carefully peel off wax paper. While hot, roll cake and towel up jelly roll-style from narrow end. Let cool on wire rack.

4 To make frosting, in a large bowl with an electric mixer, beat butter, cocoa and vanilla until creamy. Slowly add confectioners' sugar and milk until smooth. Gently unroll cake and spread ¾ cup frosting over cake. Roll cake up again, without towel. Frost outside of cake. Score cake with a fork to look like tree bark. Chill before serving. Keep refrigerated.

Test Kitchen Tip: *Since you don't need all the batter for the log, you can use it to bake cupcakes in a 350 degree oven for 15 to 18 minutes. Frost, if desired. What a bonus!*

HOLIDAY SPECIAL

Pokes
and Dumps

Tropical Island Poke Cake

You wouldn't start a conga line and give up halfway through, and we wouldn't promise you lots of tropical goodness and have it end at the frosting layer. The beauty of poke cakes is that the whole cake gets filled with flavor—in this case, a creamy coconut mixture that'll really get you up and dancing. Serve each slice with a wedge of fresh pineapple and a bright red cherry for extra fun!

Serves 15

Ingredients

1 package white cake mix

3 eggs

⅓ cup vegetable oil

2 (8-ounce) cans crushed pineapple, drained, with juice reserved (with enough water added to equal 1 cup liquid)

1 (14-ounce) can cream of coconut

1 (14-ounce) can sweetened condensed milk

1 (16-ounce) container frozen whipped topping, thawed

½ cup flaked coconut, toasted

Preparation

1 Preheat oven to 350 degrees F. Coat a 9- x 13-inch baking dish with cooking spray. In a large bowl with an electric mixer, beat cake mix, eggs, oil, and the 1 cup reserved pineapple juice and water mixture until thoroughly combined. Pour batter into baking dish.

2 Bake 25 to 30 minutes, or until a toothpick inserted in center comes out clean. Let cool 10 minutes, then poke holes in top of cake using the handle of a wooden spoon.

3 In a medium bowl, combine cream of coconut and condensed milk; mix well. Pour mixture over top of cake and into holes. Refrigerate until cooled completely.

4 In a medium bowl, combine whipped topping and crushed pineapple. Spread evenly over cake. Sprinkle with coconut and refrigerate 4 hours, or until ready to serve. Keep refrigerated.

Did You Know? *A poke cake is basically a cake that's been "poked" with the handle of a wooden spoon, shortly after it's been baked. The holes in the cake are then filled with anything from pudding and gelatin to cream cheese and ice cream toppings. The results are amazingly good!*

Peanut Butter 'n' Banana Poke Cake

If you love the insanely odd, yet incredibly good combo of peanut butter and bananas, then stop flippin' through the pages and start baking. And as if this combo itself isn't enough, we took it to a whole new level by adding the creaminess of pudding and the smokiness of bacon. We do want to warn you though, this poke cake has been known to "just disappear," so you might want to hide it in the back of the fridge until after dinner!

Serves 15

Ingredients

1 cup peanut butter, divided

1 stick [½ cup] butter, softened

4 eggs

1 package golden butter cake mix

⅔ cup water

1 [4-serving size] package instant banana cream pudding mix

2 cups milk

1 [8-ounce] container frozen whipped topping, thawed

8 slices crispy cooked bacon, crumbled

Preparation

1 Preheat oven to 350 degrees F. Coat a 9- x 13-inch baking dish with cooking spray.

2 In a large bowl with an electric mixer, beat ½ cup peanut butter and butter until creamy. Add eggs; mix well. Beat in cake mix and water until thoroughly combined. Pour into baking dish.

3 Bake 30 to 35 minutes, or until a toothpick inserted in center comes out clean. Let cool 10 minutes, then poke holes in top of cake using the handle of a wooden spoon.

4 In a medium bowl, whisk pudding mix and milk until slightly thickened. Pour mixture over cake, spreading with a spatula to fill holes. Refrigerate until cooled completely.

5 In a medium bowl, combine remaining ½ cup peanut butter and the whipped topping until well mixed. Evenly spread mixture over top of cake, then sprinkle with bacon. Refrigerate 4 hours, or until ready to serve. Keep refrigerated.

Shirley Temple Poke Cake

Whether or not you remember Shirley Temple, the famous child star of the 1930s, you've probably heard of the classic "mocktail" named after her. This super-sweet, non-alcoholic drink has been a favorite of kids of all ages since it was first introduced. Now, we've taken its signature taste and used it to make this memorable dessert that pops with color!

Serves 15

Ingredients

1 (10-ounce) jar maraschino cherries, drained, with ½ cup liquid reserved

½ cup lemon-lime soda

1 package white cake mix

3 eggs

¼ cup vegetable oil

1 cup boiling water

1 (4-serving size) package cherry-flavored gelatin mix

1 (8-ounce) container frozen whipped topping, thawed

Preparation

1 Preheat oven to 350 degrees F. Coat a 9- x 13-inch baking dish with cooking spray. In a small bowl, combine reserved ½ cup cherry liquid and soda.

2 In a large bowl with an electric mixer, beat cake mix, eggs, oil, and cherry-soda liquid until thoroughly combined. Pour batter into baking dish.

3 Bake 25 to 30 minutes, or until a toothpick inserted in center comes out clean. Let cool 10 minutes, then poke holes in top of cake using the handle of a wooden spoon. Cut cherries into quarters, then insert a piece of cherry into each of the holes.

4 In a bowl, add boiling water to gelatin mix; stir until dissolved, then slowly pour over cake and into holes. Refrigerate 4 hours or overnight. Before serving, spread whipped topping over cake and garnish with remaining cherries. Keep refrigerated.

Salted Caramel Poke Cake

What began as a trendy flavor in high-end candy shops and gourmet ice cream parlors is now a popular option almost anywhere you can find sweet treats. The combination of rich chocolate, laced with gooey caramel and accented with sea salt is an undeniably good taste sensation. If you haven't tried it yet, we urge you to do it soon! If you have, then we wouldn't be surprised if you had stopped reading at "Salted Caramel" to start baking.

Serves 15

Ingredients

1 package dark chocolate cake mix

1 cup sour cream, divided

1 cup water

⅓ cup vegetable oil

3 eggs

1 (14-ounce) jar caramel dessert topping, divided

1 stick (½ cup) butter

1 teaspoon vanilla extract

4 cups confectioners' sugar

Sea salt for sprinkling

Preparation

1 Preheat oven to 350 degrees F. Coat a 9- x 13-inch baking dish with cooking spray.

2 In a large bowl with an electric mixer, beat cake mix, ½ cup sour cream, the water, oil, and eggs until thoroughly combined. Pour batter into baking dish.

3 Bake 25 to 30 minutes, or until a toothpick inserted in center comes out clean. Let cool 10 minutes, then poke holes in top of cake using the handle of a wooden spoon. Evenly pour ¾ of the jar of caramel topping into holes of cake, reserving the rest for later. Refrigerate until cooled completely.

4 In a large bowl with an electric mixer, beat butter, remaining ½ cup sour cream, and vanilla until creamy. Slowly add in confectioners' sugar, beating until smooth. Evenly spread topping on cake. Drizzle remaining caramel topping over cake and swirl with a knife. Refrigerate 2 hours, or until ready to serve. Just before serving, sprinkle with sea salt. Keep refrigerated.

Strawberry Cheesecake Poke Cake

If your idea of the perfect cheesecake is the traditional kind with berries piled on top, then we suggest you stop flipping the pages and start preheating the oven right now. This dessert is designed just for you. It's simply sensational!

Serves 15

Ingredients

1 box white cake mix

1 cup milk

¼ cup vegetable oil

½ cup sour cream

3 eggs

1 (14-ounce) can sweetened condensed milk

1 (20-ounce) container strawberry ice cream topping syrup

1 (8-ounce) package cream cheese, softened

2 cups heavy cream

2 cups confectioners' sugar

8 strawberries, cut in half lengthwise

Preparation

1 Preheat oven to 350 degrees F. Coat a 9- x 13-inch baking dish with cooking spray.

2 In a large bowl with an electric mixer, beat cake mix, milk, oil, sour cream, and eggs until thoroughly combined; pour into baking dish.

3 Bake 28 to 30 minutes, or until toothpick inserted in center comes out clean. Cool 10 minutes, then poke holes in top of cake using the handle of a wooden spoon. Pour sweetened condensed milk over cake and into holes; let sit 5 minutes. Pour strawberry syrup over cake and into holes. Refrigerate until cooled completely.

4 In a large bowl with an electric mixer, beat cream cheese until fluffy. Add heavy cream and beat until smooth. Add confectioners' sugar and beat until stiff peaks form. Spread mixture over cake. Garnish with strawberries and refrigerate 4 hours, or until ready to serve. Keep refrigerated.

Fancy It Up: We like to top this cake with fresh strawberries for a berry-special look. If you'd like to do it too, be sure to add more strawberries to your shopping list!

Grandma's Favorite Butterscotch Poke Cake

Everyone knows a grandma or two who is famous for her love of butterscotch candies. Inspired by those sweet ladies who are always so sweet to us, we came up with a cake that any grandma would approve of (even non-grannies will love it!). Between the classic spice cake flavors and the creamy butterscotch filling, we're not sure what she's going to love best, but we do know that just one bite will put a smile on her face!

Serves 15

Ingredients

1 package spice cake mix

1 cup apple juice

⅓ cup vegetable oil

3 eggs

1 (4-serving size) package instant butterscotch pudding mix

2 cups milk

1 (8-ounce) package cream cheese, softened

1 cup confectioners' sugar

2 cups heavy cream

Preparation

1 Preheat oven to 350 degrees F. Coat a 9- x 13-inch baking dish with cooking spray.

2 In a large bowl with an electric mixer, beat cake mix, apple juice, oil, and eggs until thoroughly combined. Pour into baking dish.

3 Bake 25 to 30 minutes, or until a toothpick inserted in center comes out clean. Let cool 10 minutes, then poke holes in top of cake using the handle of a wooden spoon.

4 In a medium bowl, whisk pudding and milk just until pudding begins to thicken, but is still pourable. Pour mixture over cake, spreading with a spatula to fill holes. Refrigerate until cooled completely.

5 In a large bowl, beat cream cheese, confectioners' sugar, and heavy cream until light and fluffy. Evenly spread topping over cake. Refrigerate 4 hours, or until ready to serve. Keep refrigerated.

Finishing Touch: *We like to top each slice with a couple of gingersnap cookies right before serving.*

Death by Chocolate Poke Cake

After developing thousands of desserts here in the Test Kitchen, the one that has continually stood the test of time is our fudgy "Death by Chocolate" trifle. With that said, we decided to take all the ooey-gooey goodness that everyone loves in that dessert and turn it into a poke cake that's oh-so decadent and super simple. It's one dessert that'll soon be on your family's most requested list.

Serves 15

Ingredients

1 package devil's food cake mix

1 cup water

⅓ cup vegetable oil

3 eggs

1-½ cups chopped chocolate-covered toffee bars, divided (see Tip)

1 (14-ounce) jar hot fudge sauce, warmed

2 (4-serving size) packages instant chocolate pudding mix

3 cups milk

1 (8-ounce) container frozen whipped topping, thawed

Preparation

1 Preheat oven to 350 degrees F. Coat a 9- x 13-inch baking dish with cooking spray.

2 In a large bowl with an electric mixer, beat cake mix, water, oil, and eggs until thoroughly combined. Stir in 1 cup toffee, then pour into baking dish.

3 Bake 25 to 30 minutes, or until a toothpick inserted in center comes out clean. Let cool 10 minutes, then poke holes in top of cake using the handle of a wooden spoon. Pour hot fudge over cake, spreading with a spatula to fill holes.

4 In a large bowl, whisk pudding mix and milk until slightly thickened. Evenly spread over cake. Spread whipped topping evenly over pudding and sprinkle with remaining ½ cup toffee. Refrigerate 4 hours, or until ready to serve. Keep refrigerated.

Did You Know? *If you're wondering what chocolate-covered toffee bars are, they are best known as Heath® or Skor® bars.*

Holiday Eggnog Poke Cake

To many of us, the holidays just aren't the holidays without eggnog. There's something about the spiced, creamy, and often spiked, beverage that really gets us in the spirit of things. While a glass of eggnog is typically traditional, we think you should welcome in this year's festivities with our eggnog poke cake. We can't promise that you'll get kissed under the mistletoe, but we can assure you that there will be lots of lip-smackin' goodness in every bite!

Serves 15

Ingredients

1 package white cake mix

2-½ cups eggnog, divided

⅓ cup vegetable oil

3 eggs

1 (4-serving size) package instant vanilla pudding mix

2 tablespoons brandy (optional)

2 cups heavy cream

1 tablespoon vanilla extract

½ cup confectioners' sugar

Ground cinnamon for sprinkling

Preparation

1 Preheat oven to 350 degrees F. Coat a 9- x 13-inch baking dish with cooking spray.

2 In a large bowl with an electric mixer, beat cake mix, 1 cup eggnog, the oil, and eggs until thoroughly combined. Pour batter into baking dish.

3 Bake 25 to 30 minutes, or until a toothpick inserted in center comes out clean. Let cool 10 minutes, then poke holes in top of cake using the handle of a wooden spoon.

4 In a medium bowl, whisk pudding mix, brandy, if desired, and remaining 1-½ cups eggnog, until slightly thickened. Pour mixture over cake, spreading with a spatula to fill holes. Refrigerate until cooled completely.

5 In a large bowl, beat heavy cream, vanilla, and confectioners' sugar until stiff peaks form. Evenly spread topping over cake, then sprinkle with cinnamon. Refrigerate 4 hours, or until ready to serve. Keep refrigerated.

HOLIDAY SPECIAL

Cherry-Pineapple Dump Cake

Cherry and pineapple are no strangers to one another. These fruits are often paired together in desserts, like in an upside-down pineapple cake, as well as in savory dishes (glazed ham, anyone?). That's why it should come as no surprise that this perfect fruit duo can make a dump cake taste so extraordinary. Just wait till you dig in!

Serves 12

Ingredients

1 (21-ounce) can cherry pie filling

1 (20-ounce) can crushed pineapple, undrained

1 package yellow cake mix

1 teaspoon ground cinnamon

1 stick (½ cup) butter, cut into thin slices

½ cup chopped walnuts

Preparation

1 Preheat oven to 350 degrees F. Coat a 9- x 13-inch baking dish with cooking spray.

2 Combine pie filling, pineapple, and pineapple liquid in baking dish; mix well.

3 In a medium bowl, combine cake mix and cinnamon. Sprinkle dry cake mixture evenly over fruit mixture. Place butter slices evenly over top, then sprinkle with walnuts.

4 Bake 45 to 50 minutes, or until golden brown and bubbly. Serve piping hot right out of the oven or chilled. Keep refrigerated.

__Did You Know?__ The name "dump cake" refers to the super-easy process of making these types of cakes. While there are many variations, the basic idea is that you dump the ingredients into a baking dish, top with some butter, and bake. Most dump cakes are made with some kind of fruit filling, but there are some non-fruit versions as well.

Georgia Peach Cobbler with Brown Sugar Cream

If you're craving peach cobbler, like the kind they make in the South, but don't really want to go through all the hassle of slicing fresh peaches, then you'll love our simple shortcut version. And when you serve it bubblin' hot and topped with our homemade brown sugar whipped cream, be prepared to have your taste buds go wild with joy.

Serves 12

Ingredients

1 (21-ounce) can peach pie filling

1 (29-ounce) can sliced peaches in light syrup, undrained

1 package gluten-free yellow cake mix

½ cup oats

¼ cup plus 2 tablespoons light brown sugar, divided

1 teaspoon ground cinnamon

1 stick (½ cup) butter, cut into thin slices

1 cup heavy cream

Preparation

1 Preheat oven to 350 degrees F. Coat a 9- x 13-inch baking dish with cooking spray. Spread pie filling in baking dish. Evenly spoon peaches with the syrup over filling.

2 In a medium bowl, combine cake mix, oats, 2 tablespoons brown sugar, and the cinnamon. Evenly sprinkle mixture over peaches and top with butter.

3 Bake 40 to 45 minutes, or until golden and bubbly. Let cool 10 minutes.

4 Meanwhile, in a medium bowl, beat heavy cream and remaining ¼ cup brown sugar until soft peaks form. Spoon over warm cake and serve. Keep refrigerated.

Note: If gluten is not an issue in your diet, you can use regular cake mix.

Good For You! *We tested this with a gluten-free cake mix, but to be sure the whole recipe is truly gluten-free, always check each ingredient, as they may vary from brand to brand.*

GLUTEN FREE

Lemon-Blackberry Dump Cake

When Patty came into the Test Kitchen one day with a ton (or at least that's what it seemed like!) of fresh blackberries, we knew we had to get to work. After snacking on them as-is and using them to make pies and smoothies, we finally came up with a perfect pucker-up, summertime dump cake. The best part about this cake is that it's great for lazy days - just dump, bake, and enjoy!

Serves 12

Ingredients

5 cups fresh or frozen blackberries

½ cup sugar

Zest from ½ lemon

Juice from ½ lemon

1 package lemon cake mix

1 stick (½ cup) butter, cut into thin slices

Preparation

1 Preheat oven to 350 degrees F. Coat a 9- x 13-inch baking dish with cooking spray.

2 Spread blackberries evenly in baking dish and sprinkle with sugar and lemon zest. Drizzle lemon juice over berries; mix well, then sprinkle evenly with cake mix. Distribute butter slices evenly over top.

3 Bake 45 to 50 minutes, or until bubbly and golden. Serve piping hot right out of the oven or chilled. Keep refrigerated.

Serving Suggestion: *Sure, you can eat this as-is, but why would you want to when it's so much better spooned over a big scoop of vanilla ice cream? Trust us on this one...it's amazing.*

Apple-Cranberry Dump Cake

We've packed some of our favorite fall flavors into this dump cake that's made in your slow cooker. So now, not only can you enjoy the mouthwatering taste of fresh apples accented with tart cranberries and crunchy pecans, but you can fill your home with warm and welcoming smells, too. It's a win-win any way you look at it!

Serves 10

Ingredients

5 apples, peeled, cored, and cut into ½-inch wedges

1 cup fresh or frozen cranberries

½ cup light brown sugar

1-½ teaspoons ground cinnamon, divided

1 package yellow cake mix

¾ cup chopped pecans

1 stick [½ cup] butter, melted

1 quart vanilla ice cream

Preparation

1 Coat a 5-quart or larger slow cooker with cooking spray. Place apples, cranberries, brown sugar, and ½ teaspoon cinnamon in slow cooker; toss until evenly coated.

2 In a medium bowl, combine cake mix, pecans, and remaining 1 teaspoon cinnamon; mix well. Sprinkle over fruit and drizzle with butter.

3 Cover and cook on HIGH 2 to 2-½ hours, or until fruit is tender. Serve warm with ice cream.

Test Kitchen Tip: *This makes for a welcome addition to your Thanksgiving feast, and since it's made in a slow cooker you don't have to worry about having enough oven space. Isn't it great when things work out that way?*

SLOW COOKER

Creative Cupcakes

Totally Tempting Tiramisu Cupcakes

If you're the person who always marvels at the tiramisu in the glass case displays of fancy Italian bakeries, then you're going to love these cupcakes. They've got the same tempting flavors you love in tiramisu, but are much easier to make. So enjoy, as-is, or with a steaming cup of cappuccino. You deserve to give in to temptation every once in a while!

Makes 24

Ingredients

1 package yellow cake mix, batter prepared according to package directions

¼ cup coffee liqueur

12 ounces cream cheese, softened

1 (8-ounce) package mascarpone cheese

2-½ cups confectioners' sugar

1 teaspoon instant coffee granules

1 tablespoon warm water

Unsweetened cocoa powder for sprinkling

Preparation

1 Preheat oven to 350 degrees F. Line 24 muffin cups with paper liners.

2 Evenly divide prepared batter into paper liners. Bake according to package directions and cool completely.

3 Using a paring knife, cut out the center of each cupcake, about ½-inch wide and 1-inch deep, making sure to leave the sides and bottom intact. (See note.) Drizzle ½ teaspoon coffee liqueur over the inside of each cupcake.

4 In a large bowl with an electric mixer, beat cream cheese and mascarpone cheese until creamy. Slowly add confectioners' sugar and beat until smooth. In a small bowl, dissolve coffee granules in water, then add to the cheese mixture; mix well.

5 Evenly fill center and frost each cupcake with cheese mixture. Sprinkle with cocoa powder. Keep refrigerated.

Decisions, Decisions: *You could just toss out the inside pieces that you scooped out or (better yet!) if you have some extra frosting, you could mix it with the cake pieces, roll into 1-inch balls and nibble on them when no one's looking!*

Ooey-Gooey Campfire Cupcakes

Don't start gathering your marshmallow roasting sticks just yet! These cupcakes aren't made over a campfire, they're baked right in your oven. Of course, it wouldn't be right to call them campfire cupcakes if they didn't have lots of ooey-gooey yumminess, so you can bet there's plenty of that. We've just made it easier for you to grab and go!

Makes 24

Ingredients

1 package devil's food cake mix

1 cup water

⅓ cup vegetable oil

3 eggs

2 teaspoons vanilla extract

48 large marshmallows, divided

1 (16-ounce) container chocolate frosting

3 graham cracker sheets, each cut into 8 equal pieces

Preparation

1 Preheat oven to 350 degrees F. Line 24 muffin cups with paper liners.

2 In a large bowl with an electric mixer, beat cake mix, water, oil, eggs, and vanilla until thoroughly combined. Evenly divide batter into paper liners. Place 1 marshmallow in center of each cupcake.

3 Bake 18 to 20 minutes, or until cake is set. Remove from oven and immediately push another marshmallow into center of each cupcake. Return to oven 2 minutes, or until marshmallows begin to melt. Let cool completely.

4 Frost cupcakes, then garnish with graham cracker pieces.

Finishing Touch: *To add a little more crunch to every bite, we like to crumble an extra graham cracker or two to sprinkle on top of each cupcake.*

Summer's Best Orange Cream Cupcakes

Remember those orange and vanilla melt-in-your-mouth ice cream bars that you would buy from the ice cream man? Who can forget them? They were (and still are!) one of our favorite summertime treats. Well, we took that same tasty duo and turned it into a cupcake that's bursting with flavor. Now you can enjoy the flavors of summertime, anytime!

Makes 20

Ingredients

1 package orange cake mix

3 eggs

⅓ cup vegetable oil

1 tablespoon orange zest

Juice of 1 orange, plus enough water to make 1 cup liquid total

FROSTING

1 (8-ounce) package cream cheese, softened

1 stick (½ cup) butter, softened

1 teaspoon vanilla extract

5 cups confectioners' sugar

Preparation

1 Preheat oven to 350 degrees F. Place paper liners in 20 muffin cups.

2 In a large bowl with an electric mixer, beat cake mix, eggs, oil, orange zest, and orange juice and water mixture until combined. Evenly divide batter into paper liners.

3 Bake 15 to 20 minutes, or until a toothpick comes out clean. Let cool completely.

4 To make frosting, in a large bowl with an electric mixer, beat cream cheese, butter, and vanilla until creamy. Slowly add confectioners' sugar, beating until smooth.

5 Cut cupcakes in half horizontally. Place a spoonful of cream cheese frosting on top of bottom half of each cupcake. Replace cupcake tops. Frost cupcakes with remaining frosting. Keep refrigerated.

Fancy It Up: After frosting the cupcakes, grate some additional orange zest over them for an extra blast of orangey goodness.

Smoky Bacon Cupcakes with Maple Frosting

Our inspiration for these cupcakes comes from a favorite breakfast combination—bacon and pancakes. Let's be honest, bacon tastes extra-good once some of the sweet maple syrup from the pancakes has oozed onto it. That's why we had to put the two flavors together! And when you decorate each one with even more bacon, all the better. We're not saying these cupcakes are a great breakfast idea, but who are we to judge?

Makes 24

Ingredients

1 package yellow cake mix

1 cup water

⅓ cup vegetable oil

3 eggs

1 tablespoon maple syrup

12 slices crispy cooked bacon, divided
(4 slices crumbled,
8 slices cut into 1-inch pieces)

FROSTING

1-½ sticks (¾ cup) butter, softened

¼ cup maple syrup

4 cups confectioners' sugar

2 tablespoons milk

Preparation

1 Preheat oven to 350 degrees F. Line 24 muffin cups with paper liners.

2 In a large bowl with an electric mixer, beat cake mix, water, oil, eggs, and 1 tablespoon maple syrup until thoroughly combined. Stir crumbled bacon into batter. Evenly divide batter into paper liners.

3 Bake 15 to 18 minutes, or until a toothpick comes out clean; let cool completely.

4 To make frosting, in a large bowl with an electric mixer, beat butter and ¼ cup maple syrup until creamy. Gradually add confectioners' sugar and milk, beating until smooth. Frost cupcakes. Decorate each cupcake with a couple of 1-inch pieces of bacon. Keep refrigerated.

Did You Know? *The best way to bring cupcakes to a party is in a cupcake carrier. They come in all shapes, colors, and sizes. This one looks like a big plastic egg carton. Pretty cool, huh?!*

Fudgy Cake Cones with Ice Cream Frosting

We've got a different kind of ice cream cone for you to enjoy this summer, and this is one you can take your time to eat, since there'll be no ice cream drips to worry about! That's because they're actually fudgy cupcakes baked right inside the cone. When you top them with our vanilla ice cream frosting and colorful sprinkles, they look just like the real thing!

Makes 24

Ingredients

24 flat-bottomed ice cream cones

1 package chocolate cake mix, batter prepared according to package directions

½ cup hot fudge ice cream topping

¼ cup rainbow sprinkles, for garnish

FROSTING

1 stick (½ cup) butter, melted

1 teaspoon vanilla extract

½ cup vanilla ice cream, melted

4 cups confectioners' sugar

Preparation

1 Preheat oven to 350 degrees F. Place ice cream cones in muffin cups and spoon 1 tablespoon prepared batter into each one. Add 1 teaspoon hot fudge to each, then cover with another tablespoon of batter.

2 Bake 20 to 22 minutes, or until a toothpick inserted in center comes out clean. Let cool completely.

3 To make frosting, in a large bowl with an electric mixer, beat all ingredients until smooth. Frost cupcakes and garnish with sprinkles. Keep refrigerated. (See Tip.)

Test Kitchen Tip: *Adding a little dollop of frosting to the bottom of each finished cone will help them stay upright when refrigerating or serving.*

Lemon Curd Cupcakes with Raspberry Frosting

Hello, sunshine! If you're craving a burst of summery goodness, then you've come to the right page. These cupcakes, stuffed with creamy lemon curd and topped with a rich raspberry frosting are sure to brighten up your day. And if you know someone who needs a little brightening up, then we recommend you share with them. They're known to help turn frowns upside-down!

Makes 24

Ingredients

1 package lemon cake mix, batter prepared according to package directions

1 (10-ounce) jar lemon curd (see Note)

FROSTING

1-½ sticks (¾ cup) butter, softened

1 teaspoon vanilla extract

⅛ teaspoon salt

½ cup seedless raspberry preserves

4 cups confectioners' sugar

Preparation

1 Preheat oven to 350 degrees F. Line 24 muffin cups with paper liners.

2 Evenly divide batter into paper liners. Place 1 teaspoon lemon curd in center of batter.

3 Bake 15 to 18 minutes, or until set; let cool completely.

4 To make frosting, in a large bowl with an electric mixer, beat butter, vanilla, and salt until creamy. Add raspberry preserves and gradually beat in confectioners' sugar until smooth; frost cupcakes. Keep refrigerated.

Note: You can find lemon curd in the market next to all the jams and jellies.

Fancy It Up: *For that extra-special touch, top each cupcake with some freshly grated lemon zest, a raspberry, and a sprig of mint.*

Peanut Butter Cup Cupcakes

Peanut butter cups are one of the most popular candies in America. There's just no denying that we love the combination of decadent chocolate stuffed with creamy peanut butter. That's why we knew we had to take that to-die-for combo and put it into a cupcake. As you can imagine, the taste is truly outrageous.

Makes 24

Ingredients

1 package chocolate cake mix

1 cup milk

4 eggs

¼ cup vegetable oil

¼ cup sour cream

24 mini peanut butter cups, frozen, plus 12 for garnish

FROSTING

1-½ cups creamy peanut butter

1 stick (½ cup) butter, softened

2 cups confectioners' sugar

1-½ teaspoons vanilla extract

½ cup heavy cream

Preparation

1 Preheat oven to 350 degrees F. Line 24 muffin cups with paper liners.

2 In a large bowl with an electric mixer, combine cake mix, milk, eggs, oil, and sour cream until thoroughly combined. Evenly divide batter into paper liners. Place a peanut butter cup in the center of the batter in each cup and gently press down a little. (The tops of the candy should still be showing.)

3 Bake 18 to 22 minutes, or until cake is set. Let cool completely.

4 To make frosting, in a large bowl with an electric mixer, beat together peanut butter and butter until smooth. Slowly add confectioners' sugar and vanilla and beat until smooth. Add cream, beating until light and fluffy. Frost cupcakes. Cut remaining 12 peanut butter cups in half and garnish. Keep refrigerated.

Southern Hospitality Sweet Tea Cupcakes

Nothing says Southern hospitality like a welcoming host bringing out a pitcher of ice-cold sweet tea. Inspired by their graciousness (and that delicious tea!) we came up with this cupcake that has sweet iced tea baked right in them! To round them out, we finished each cupcake with a generous amount of our homemade, lemony buttercream frosting. Share with the neighbors, some friends, or your loved ones and help spread some sweet, Southern-style cheer.

Makes 24

Ingredients

1 package white cake mix

1-¼ cups sweetened iced tea

⅓ cup vegetable oil

3 eggs

1 teaspoon lemon zest

Fresh mint for garnish

Lemon wedges for garnish

FROSTING

1 stick (½ cup) butter, softened

3 tablespoons lemon juice

1 tablespoon milk

3 drops yellow food color

5 cups confectioners' sugar

Preparation

1 Preheat oven to 350 degrees F. Place 24 paper liners in muffin cups.

2 In a large bowl, beat cake mix, iced tea, oil, eggs, and lemon zest until thoroughly combined. Evenly divide batter into paper liners.

3 Bake 15 to 18 minutes, or until a toothpick comes out clean. Let cool completely.

4 Meanwhile, in a large bowl with an electric mixer, beat butter until creamy. Add lemon juice, milk, and food color; slowly beat in confectioners' sugar until smooth.

5 Frost cupcakes and garnish with mint and lemon. Keep refrigerated.

So Many Options: *While we made these with a traditional-style Southern sweet tea, you can always use any type of tea you prefer, including green tea or decaffeinated tea. The results will be just as welcoming!*

Toffee Crunch Cupcakes

We hope you're ready to get crunching because these cupcakes are full of crunchy, tasty, toffee bits! Not only do we stir the candy pieces right into the batter, but we also sprinkle them on top of our homemade, dark chocolate frosting. This is the cupcake that every toffee lover dreams about.

Makes 24

Ingredients

1 package gluten-free yellow cake mix

1 cup water

⅓ cup vegetable oil

1 teaspoon vanilla extract

3 eggs

½ cup chocolate toffee bits, plus ¼ cup for garnish (see Tip)

FROSTING

1-½ sticks (¾ cup) butter, melted

¾ cup dark cocoa powder

2 teaspoons vanilla extract

6 cups confectioners' sugar

⅓ cup plus 1 tablespoon milk

Preparation

1   Preheat oven to 350 degrees F. Place 24 paper liners in muffin cups.

2   In a large bowl with an electric mixer, beat cake mix, water, oil, 1 teaspoon vanilla, and eggs until thoroughly combined. Stir in ½ cup toffee bits. Evenly divide batter into paper liners.

3   Bake 15 to 18 minutes, or until a toothpick comes out clean. Let cool completely.

4   To make frosting, in a large bowl, combine butter, cocoa powder, and 2 teaspoons vanilla; mix well. Slowly beat in confectioners' sugar and milk until smooth. Frost cupcakes and sprinkle with remaining toffee bits. Keep refrigerated.

Test Kitchen Tip: *While many store-bought toffee bits are gluten-free, it's always a good idea to double-check all your ingredients, since this can vary from brand to brand.*

GLUTEN FREE

Circus Cupcakes with Marshmallow Frosting

Ladies and gentlemen! Boys and girls! We invite you to experience the greatest and tastiest cupcake circus on earth! Our dazzling Circus Cupcakes deliver lots of fun all the way from the strawberry-colored cake filled with plenty of sprinkles to the fluffy marshmallow frosting that sets the stage for your favorite animal cracker friends! These cupcakes are great for the young and the young-at-heart!

Makes 24

Ingredients

1 package strawberry cake mix

1 cup milk

⅓ cup vegetable oil

3 eggs

4 tablespoons rainbow sprinkles, divided

24 animal cracker cookies

FROSTING

2 sticks (1 cup) butter, softened

1 cup marshmallow creme

1 teaspoon vanilla extract

4 cups confectioners' sugar

Preparation

1 Preheat oven to 350 degrees F. Place 24 paper liners in muffin cups.

2 In a large bowl with an electric mixer, beat cake mix, milk, oil, and eggs until thoroughly combined. Gently stir in 3 tablespoons sprinkles. Evenly divide batter into paper liners.

3 Bake 15 to 20 minutes, or until a toothpick comes out clean. Let cool completely.

4 To make frosting, in a large bowl with an electric mixer, beat butter, marshmallow creme, and vanilla until creamy. Slowly add confectioners' sugar and beat until smooth. Frost cupcakes. Garnish with animal crackers and remaining 1 tablespoon sprinkles. Keep refrigerated.

Baba Au Rhum

If you're thinking, "What the heck is a Baba au Rhum?" you're probably not alone! It's a classic French pastry that's soaked with liquor and filled with a creamy custard or whipped cream. Our shortcut version starts with a boxed cake mix and uses instant vanilla pudding, which means we can whip these up in no time! When you serve them, get ready for lots of "C'est si bon!" (that's "OOH IT'S SO GOOD!!®" in French).

Serves 12

Ingredients

1 package yellow cake mix, batter prepared according to package directions

1 (4-serving size) package instant vanilla pudding mix

1-½ cups cold milk

1 cup water

1 cup sugar

½ cup light rum

1 cup frozen whipped topping, thawed

12 maraschino cherries

Preparation

1 Preheat oven to 350 degrees F. Bake batter, without paper liners, according to package directions for 2 dozen cupcakes; let cool. [See Tip.]

2 Meanwhile, in a medium bowl, whisk pudding mix and milk 1 minute, or until smooth. Cover pudding and chill.

3 In a small bowl, combine water, sugar, and rum, stirring until sugar is dissolved; set aside.

4 Place 12 cupcakes in a 9- x 13-inch baking dish. Slowly pour rum mixture over cupcakes. Cover and chill 1 hour, allowing liquid to soak into cupcakes. Remove cupcakes from rum mixture and place upside down on a serving platter. Using a knife, make 2 cuts halfway through each cupcake, forming an "X." Spoon pudding evenly over cuts in each cupcake, opening up cupcakes a bit. Top each with a dollop of whipped topping and a cherry. Keep refrigerated.

Test Kitchen Tip: *Since the batter makes 24 cupcakes and you only need 12 of them for this recipe, feel free to freeze the rest. When you're craving these again, all you have to do is whip up an extra batch of the cream filling and you're good to go!*

Chocolate Chip Cheesecake Cupcakes

If you had to decide between a creamy cheesecake and a super moist chocolate cake, what would you choose? We didn't think it was fair to put you in that position, so we came up with a decadent chocolate cupcake that features a chocolate chip cheesecake filling. Ah, if only everything in life was that simple.

Makes 30

Ingredients

1 package chocolate cake mix, batter prepared according to package directions

1 (8-ounce) package cream cheese, softened

⅓ cup sugar

1 egg

¼ cup mini chocolate chips, plus 2 tablespoons for garnish

1 (16-ounce) container cream cheese frosting

Preparation

1 Preheat oven to 350 degrees F. Line 30 muffin cups with paper liners. Spoon half the prepared batter evenly into muffin cups.

2 In a large bowl with an electric mixer, beat cream cheese and sugar until light and fluffy. Beat in the egg, then stir in ¼ cup chocolate chips. Drop 1 teaspoon cream cheese mixture into each muffin cup, then evenly top each with remaining batter.

3 Bake 15 to 18 minutes, or until a toothpick comes out clean.

4 Let cool completely, then frost cupcakes. Sprinkle with remaining 2 tablespoons chocolate chips. Keep refrigerated.

Black Bottom Cookie Cupcakes

You know what would go great with a black-and-white-themed party? These cupcakes with a surprise cream-filled cookie buried inside each one! Plus, the homemade buttercream frosting is the perfect complement to this classic flavor combination. You can bet everyone will be RSVP'ing to your party. (And even if you aren't having a party, these are still amazing!)

Makes 24

Ingredients

1 (16.6-ounce) package cream-filled chocolate sandwich cookies, divided (see Tip)

1 package white cake mix, batter prepared according to package instructions

FROSTING

2 sticks (1 cup) butter, softened

2 teaspoons vanilla extract

6 cups confectioners' sugar

3 tablespoons milk

Preparation

1 Preheat oven to 350 degrees F. Line 24 muffin cups with black and white paper liners. Place a cookie in bottom of each liner; set aside.

2 Evenly divide prepared batter into paper liners.

3 Bake 15 to 18 minutes, or until a toothpick comes out clean. Let cool completely.

4 To make frosting, in a large bowl with an electric mixer, beat butter and vanilla until creamy. Slowly add confectioners' sugar and milk, and beat until light and fluffy. Frost cupcakes. Cut 12 cookies in half with a sharp knife, and place half a cookie on top of each cupcake. Keep refrigerated.

Test Kitchen Tip: *Although there are many chocolate sandwich cookies to choose from, we tested these with cookies that were double-stuffed.*

All-American Stacked Cupcakes

Show off your patriotism and your tasty baking skills with these American-themed cupcakes. They're the perfect treat to make for a Fourth of July party or for welcoming home a beloved soldier. We can't think of a better way to express our pride for the USA than by sharing great food with great people in this great country.

Makes 20

Ingredients

1 package white cake mix, batter prepared according to package directions

20 drops red food color

20 drops blue food color

Blue and red colored sugar for garnish (see Tip)

FROSTING

1 stick (½ cup) butter, softened

¼ cup milk

1-½ teaspoons vanilla extract

6 cups confectioners' sugar

Preparation

1 Preheat oven to 350 degrees F. Place 20 paper liners in muffin cups.

2 Evenly divide prepared batter into 2 bowls. Add red food color to one bowl of batter and mix until blended. Add blue food color to remaining batter and mix until blended. Evenly divide batter into paper liners, making 10 red cupcakes and 10 blue cupcakes.

3 Bake 15 to 20 minutes, or until a toothpick comes out clean. Let cool completely.

4 To make frosting, in a large bowl with an electric mixer, beat butter, milk, and vanilla until creamy. Slowly add confectioners' sugar, beating until smooth.

5 Cut each cupcake in half horizontally. Evenly spread half the frosting on bottom of cupcakes, then place opposite color cupcake top on top of the frosting, as shown. Frost cupcakes with remaining frosting; sprinkle with colored sugar. Keep refrigerated.

Test Kitchen Tip: *You can make your own colored sugar by simply combining 1/4 cup sugar and 1 to 2 drops food color in a resealable storage bag. Just shake it until it's the right color!*

HOLIDAY SPECIAL

Root Beer Float Cupcakes

For everyone who loves the classic flavor of a good old-fashioned root beer float, these cupcakes are just for you. You can even use your favorite brand of root beer to make them. And don't worry, we didn't forget to put in the vanilla ice cream - it's in the frosting!

Makes 24

Ingredients

1 package German chocolate cake mix

1-¼ cups root beer

¼ cup vegetable oil

3 eggs

FROSTING

2 tablespoons butter, melted

1 teaspoon vanilla extract

2 tablespoons root beer

⅓ cup vanilla ice cream, softened

4 cups confectioners' sugar

Preparation

1 Preheat oven to 350 degrees F. Place 24 paper liners in muffin cups.

2 In a large bowl with an electric mixer, beat cake mix, 1-¼ cups root beer, the oil, and eggs until thoroughly combined. Evenly divide batter into paper liners.

3 Bake 15 to 20 minutes, or until a toothpick comes out clean. Let cool completely.

4 To make frosting, in a large bowl with an electric mixer, beat all ingredients until smooth; frost cupcakes. Keep refrigerated.

Finishing Touch: *We thought it was fun to garnish each one with a straw and a gummi candy to give it a soda shoppe look. How fun is that?!*

White Winter Wonderland Cupcakes

Whether you make these to celebrate the first snowfall of the year or to serve at a holiday party, we know they'll be a hit. Adding sour cream to the batter makes them decadently rich, while the homemade white chocolate frosting really adds a wonderful winterland touch. We hope you're ready to have a flurry of fun!

Makes 24

Ingredients

1 package white cake mix

½ cup sour cream

1 cup water

⅓ cup vegetable oil

3 eggs

¾ cup white chocolate chips

White decorating sugar for garnish

FROSTING

¾ cup white chocolate chips

¼ cup heavy cream

2 sticks (1 cup) butter, softened

5 cups confectioners' sugar

Preparation

1 Preheat oven to 350 degrees F. Line 24 muffin cups with paper liners.

2 In a large bowl with an electric mixer, beat cake mix, sour cream, water, oil, and eggs until thoroughly combined; stir in ¾ cup white chocolate chips. Evenly divide batter into paper liners.

3 Bake 15 to 18 minutes, or until a toothpick comes out clean; let cool completely.

4 To make frosting, in a medium microwave-safe bowl, combine ¾ cup white chocolate chips and the heavy cream. Microwave 60 to 75 seconds or until smooth, stirring occasionally; let cool slightly.

5 In a large bowl with an electric mixer, beat butter until creamy. Mix in white chocolate until thoroughly combined. To make frosting, in and beat until frosting is light and fluffy. Frost cupcakes, then garnish with decorating sugar. Keep refrigerated.

Finishing Touch: *To give these an extra winter wonderland feel, top each with a snowflake icing decoration that you can pick up at your market or craft store.*

HOLIDAY SPECIAL

Mile-High Cracker Jack® Cupcakes

You won't find a little toy hidden inside these cupcakes, but who's going to be thinking about toys when they've got this mile-high treat in front of them? With the crunch of everyone's favorite snack mix and lots of gooey chocolate richness, this cupcake is sure to impress even the toughest of critics.

Makes 24

Ingredients

1 cup semi-sweet chocolate chips

1 package chocolate cake mix, divided

1 cup water

⅓ cup vegetable oil

3 eggs

1 (16-ounce) container chocolate frosting

2 (1-ounce) packages Cracker Jack® (caramel coated popcorn and peanuts)

½ cup hot fudge, warmed

Preparation

1 Preheat oven to 350 degrees F. Line 24 muffin cups with paper liners.

2 In a small bowl, toss chocolate chips with 1 teaspoon of the cake mix until evenly coated; set aside.

3 In a large bowl with an electric mixer, beat remaining cake mix, water, oil, and eggs until thoroughly combined. Stir in chocolate chips. Evenly divide batter into paper liners.

4 Bake 15 to 20 minutes, or until a toothpick comes out clean. Let cool completely.

5 Top each cupcake with a dollop of frosting, pile on some Cracker Jack® popcorn and peanuts, and repeat layers, as shown. Drizzle with hot fudge and dig in.

Bars 'n' Squares 'n' Such

Apricot Almond Crumble Bars

Years ago we created a bar recipe very similar to this one, except it was made from scratch and required a whole lot of ingredients. Not to mention, the dough was temperamental. Finally, after many attempts, we found a way to recreate its great taste with a fool-proof method. We even cut the number of ingredients needed in half, since we start off with an off-the-shelf cake mix. Now you get to reap the rewards of our sweet success.

Serves 24

Ingredients

1 (8-ounce) package cream cheese, softened

2 tablespoons sugar

1 package yellow cake mix, divided

1 egg

1 teaspoon almond extract

½ cup finely chopped almonds

1 stick (½ cup) butter, melted

1 (12-ounce) jar apricot preserves

Preparation

1 Preheat oven to 350 degrees F. Coat a 9- x 13-inch baking dish with cooking spray.

2 In a medium bowl with an electric mixer, beat the cream cheese, sugar, 2 tablespoons cake mix, egg, and almond extract until creamy. Set aside.

3 In a large bowl with an electric mixer, beat remaining cake mix, the almonds, and butter until crumbly. Reserve 1 cup dough for the topping. Press remaining dough into bottom of baking dish. Spread the preserves evenly over the dough. Gently spread cream cheese mixture over the preserves. Crumble the reserved dough over the cream cheese layer.

4 Bake 30 to 35 minutes, or until golden brown and filling is set. Let cool, then cut into bars. Keep refrigerated.

Sweet Potato Cake with Marshmallow Frosting

You know the sweet potato casserole that's covered in toasty, melted marshmallows and is a must-have every Thanksgiving? That's the one that inspired this cake. We took those yummy flavors and turned them into a dessert that can be served as part of your holiday spread or at your weeknight dinner table. Oh, and just wait until you taste our marshmallow cream frosting—it's heavenly.

Serves 15

Ingredients

1 package gluten-free yellow cake mix

¾ cup milk

⅓ cup vegetable oil

3 eggs

1 (15-ounce) can sweet potatoes, drained and mashed

1 teaspoon ground cinnamon

1 teaspoon nutmeg

Candied pecans for garnish

FROSTING

1-¼ cups marshmallow creme

4 ounces cream cheese, softened

4 cups confectioners' sugar

¼ teaspoon ground cinnamon

1 teaspoon vanilla extract

Preparation

1 Preheat oven to 350 degrees F. Coat a 10- x 15-inch rimmed baking sheet with cooking spray.

2 In a large bowl with an electric mixer, beat cake mix, milk, oil, eggs, sweet potatoes, 1 teaspoon cinnamon, and nutmeg until thoroughly combined. Pour batter evenly onto baking sheet. Bake 15 to 20 minutes, or until a toothpick inserted in center comes out clean. Let cool completely.

3 To make frosting, in a large bowl with an electric mixer, beat marshmallow creme and cream cheese until smooth. Slowly add in confectioners' sugar, ¼ teaspoon cinnamon, and vanilla, and beat until thoroughly combined. Frost cake and garnish with candied pecans. Keep refrigerated.

Change It Up: *To ensure that this is truly gluten-free, make sure that all the ingredients used are gluten-free. If you are not concerned about gluten, simply use a regular cake mix.*

GLUTEN FREE

Share-Worthy Cannoli Bars

We did it! We found an easy way to deliver the taste of an Old World cannoli with the convenience of semi-homemade baking, and it just so happens to be perfect for sharing. Even the most devoted cannoli lover won't be able to pass up one of these bars. They'll still be able to enjoy the crisp-crunch of the cannoli shells too!

Serves 20

Ingredients

1 package white cake mix

¾ teaspoon ground cinnamon

1 cup water

⅓ cup vegetable oil

3 eggs

5 mini cannoli shells, coarsely crushed, for garnish

1 teaspoon mini chocolate chips for garnish

Confectioners' sugar for sprinkling

FROSTING

1 (8-ounce) container mascarpone cheese

1 cup ricotta cheese

1 teaspoon vanilla extract

1-½ cups confectioners' sugar

⅓ cup mini chocolate chips

Preparation

1 Preheat oven to 350 degrees F. Coat a 10- x 15-inch rimmed baking sheet with cooking spray.

2 In a large bowl with an electric mixer, beat cake mix, cinnamon, water, oil, and eggs until thoroughly combined. Pour batter evenly onto baking sheet.

3 Bake 15 to 20 minutes, or until a toothpick inserted in center comes out clean. Let cool completely.

4 To make frosting, in a large bowl with an electric mixer, beat mascarpone, ricotta cheese, and vanilla until creamy. Slowly add 1-½ cups confectioners' sugar and beat until smooth. Stir in ⅓ cup chocolate chips. Spread frosting evenly over cake.

5 Sprinkle with crushed cannoli shells and 1 teaspoon chocolate chips. Keep refrigerated. When ready to serve, sprinkle with extra confectioners' sugar right before cutting.

New-Fashioned Banana Pudding Cake

What happens when you take old-fashioned flavors and make them in a new-fashioned way? You'll have to bake this cake to find out! You see, we took all the creaminess and yummy banana flavor of a traditional Southern-style banana pudding and paired it with a freshly baked vanilla cake to create this jaw-dropping dessert. Oh, and of course, we did it by using some tasty shortcut ingredients. We bet even "memaw" will be impressed.

Serves 15

Ingredients

1 box vanilla cake mix

1 (4-serving size) package instant vanilla pudding mix

½ cup vegetable oil

1 cup water

3 eggs

1 teaspoon vanilla extract

1 (12-ounce) package vanilla wafer cookies, with 2 cookies crushed and reserved for garnish

1 (4-serving size) package instant banana cream pudding mix

1 cup milk

1 (16-ounce) container frozen whipped topping, thawed, divided

Preparation

1 Preheat oven to 350 degrees F. Coat a 9- x 13-inch baking dish with cooking spray.

2 In a large bowl with an electric mixer, beat cake mix, vanilla pudding mix, oil, water, eggs, and vanilla until thoroughly combined. Pour batter into baking dish. Place cookies in a single layer over top of batter. Gently push more cookies into batter, lining sides of baking dish.

3 Bake 25 to 30 minutes, or until a toothpick inserted in center comes out clean. Let cool completely.

4 In a medium bowl, whisk banana cream pudding mix and milk until thickened. Fold in 2 cups whipped topping until thoroughly combined. Spread evenly over cake. Dollop cake with remaining whipped topping and garnish with reserved crushed vanilla wafers. Refrigerate at least 2 hours before serving. Keep refrigerated.

Finishing Touch: *Feel free to "go bananas" and top each portion with a banana slice. To keep them from browning, just dip each slice in a bit of lemon juice before topping.*

German Chocolate Cheesecake Squares

When we think of incredible dessert duos, we think of the classics like cookies and milk, ice cream and pie, and, of course, peanut butter and chocolate. But now, let us introduce you to a new combo that we know you're going to love – a mashup of cheesecake and chocolate cake. And not just any chocolate cake! If you're going to go big, you've got to go with German chocolate cake. Every bite is truly decadent!

Serves 20

Ingredients

1 package German chocolate cake mix

4 eggs, divided

1 stick (½ cup) butter, melted

½ cup chopped pecans, toasted

1 cup chocolate chips

1 (8-ounce) package cream cheese, softened

3 cups confectioners' sugar

Preparation

1 Preheat oven to 325 degrees F. Coat a 9- x 13-inch baking dish with cooking spray.

2 In a large bowl, stir together cake mix, 1 egg, the butter, pecans, and chocolate chips; press mixture evenly into baking dish. The mixture will be the consistency of cookie dough.

3 In another bowl, with an electric mixer, beat cream cheese and the remaining 3 eggs until creamy; slowly add confectioners' sugar, beating until smooth. Spoon mixture evenly over batter.

4 Bake 45 to 50 minutes, or until a toothpick inserted in center comes out clean. When cool, cut into squares. Keep refrigerated.

Better-than-the-Bakery Crumb Cake

A good crumb cake has to be super moist and topped with big, buttery crumbs. Up until now, you may have only ever experienced this kind of perfection from your favorite bakery. But now that you've got this recipe in front of you, we think it's time for some friendly competition. How about you whip up this crumb cake and discover for yourself what we mean by "Better-than-the-Bakery"?

Serves 15

Ingredients

1 package yellow cake mix

¾ cup vegetable oil

¾ cup water

3 eggs

1 teaspoon vanilla extract

TOPPING

2 cups all-purpose flour

1 cup sugar

2 sticks (½ pound) butter, slightly softened

2 teaspoons ground cinnamon

Preparation

1 Preheat oven to 350 degrees F. Coat a 10- x 15-inch rimmed baking sheet with cooking spray.

2 In a large bowl with an electric mixer, beat cake mix, oil, water, eggs, and vanilla until thoroughly combined. Pour batter evenly onto baking sheet.

3 To make topping, in a medium bowl with a fork or pastry cutter, combine topping ingredients until coarse crumbs form. Evenly sprinkle over batter and bake 25 to 30 minutes, or until a toothpick inserted in center comes out clean. Let cool, then cut into squares.

Test Kitchen Tip: *The key to a great crumb topping is to make sure that you end up with large crumbs when you combine the butter with the sugar and flour. If you overmix it, it'll lose its crumbly goodness.*

Lemon Lime Soda Pop Cake

How could we not include an easy version of the classic 7Up® cake in this book? And for those of you who haven't had the pleasure of tasting it before, you're in for a treat. Not only does the soda pop add a fresh lemon-lime taste to the cake, but the carbonation makes the batter nice and light. This cake is sure to leave you bubbling over with joy!

Serves 15

Ingredients

1 package lemon cake mix

2 eggs

1 cup lemon-lime soda

1 teaspoon grated lime zest

Confectioners' sugar for sprinkling

Preparation

1 Preheat oven to 350 degrees F. Coat a 9- x 13-inch baking dish with cooking spray.

2 In a large bowl with an electric mixer, beat all ingredients, except confectioners' sugar, until thoroughly combined. Pour into baking dish.

3 Bake 25 to 30 minutes, or until a toothpick inserted in center comes out clean. Let cool completely. When ready to serve, sprinkle with confectioners' sugar.

Finishing Touch: *For an added burst of citrus, garnish your cake with some extra lime zest.*

No-Worries Chocolate Bikini Cake

When it's time to put away the baggy sweatshirts and dig out our bathing suits, many of us look for ways to lighten things up. That sounds like a good plan, yet it's hard to give up desserts. No worries; since this cake starts with a sugar-free cake mix and is made with low-fat Greek yogurt, which makes it really rich and moist. Even when we finish it off with whipped topping and hot fudge it only has 126 calories per serving.

Serves 15

Ingredients

1 package sugar-free chocolate cake mix

1 cup water

½ cup low-fat Greek vanilla yogurt

3 eggs

1 (8-ounce) container low-fat frozen whipped topping, thawed

¾ cup sugar-free hot fudge, warmed

Preparation

1 Preheat oven to 350 degrees F. Coat a 9- x 13-inch baking dish with cooking spray.

2 In a large bowl with an electric mixer, beat cake mix, water, yogurt, and eggs until thoroughly combined. Pour batter into baking dish.

3 Bake 25 to 30 minutes, or until a toothpick inserted in center comes out clean. Let cool.

4 Spread whipped topping evenly over cake. Spoon warmed hot fudge into a resealable plastic bag, then snip off one small corner of bag with scissors. Drizzle fudge in 8 straight lines lengthwise over whipped topping. Gently drag a butter knife across the lines to create a fancy look. (See photo.) Keep refrigerated.

LIGHTER OPTION

Summer Picnic Watermelon Cake

Nothing says summer like eating slices of juicy watermelon under a big shady tree, but instead of stuffing your picnic basket with a whole melon, we've come up with a unique and easy way to enjoy this summertime favorite. We've baked the watermelon flavor right into our cake! Now, you can enjoy a refreshing slice of cake that tastes like a watermelon and sort of looks like one too. You don't even have to worry about spitting out the "seeds"!

Serves 15

Ingredients

⅓ cup mini chocolate chips plus extra for garnish

1 package white cake mix, divided

1 (4-serving size) package watermelon-flavored gelatin mix

1-¼ cups water

2 eggs

⅓ cup canola oil

1 (16-ounce) container vanilla frosting

10 drops green food color

Preparation

1 Preheat oven to 350 degrees F. Coat a 9- x 13-inch baking dish with cooking spray.

2 In a small bowl, toss ⅓ cup chocolate chips with 1 teaspoon of the dry cake mix until evenly coated; set aside. (See Note.)

3 In a large bowl with an electric mixer, beat the remaining cake mix, the gelatin mix, water, eggs, and oil until thoroughly combined. Gently fold in coated chocolate chips, then pour into baking dish. Bake 25 to 30 minutes, or until a toothpick inserted in center comes out clean. Let cool completely.

4 In a medium bowl, combine frosting and food color until thoroughly mixed. Evenly spread frosting over top of cake and garnish with additional chocolate chips.

Note: The reason we toss the chocolate chips with the dry cake mix is that it prevents the chips from falling to the bottom of the batter when baking.

Test Kitchen Tip: *Depending on where you live, you may find that watermelon gelatin is only available seasonally. If that's the case, we suggest that you stock up on it when you come across it. If you can't locate it, you can always make this cake using strawberry gelatin. No worries – it's still yummy!*

Blueberry Coffee Cake Bars

Bake these coffee cake bars any time you want your family out of bed and at the breakfast table. The smell alone will get them to rise and shine. Serve them with a glass of OJ or freshly brewed coffee, and you've set the tone for a perfect day. And if, by chance, this doesn't disappear in the morning, it's just as tasty as an after-dinner dessert.

Serves 15

Ingredients

1 package white cake mix

6 tablespoons butter, melted

1-¼ cups quick-cooking oats, divided

2 eggs

1 (21-ounce) can blueberry pie filling

2 tablespoons butter, softened

¼ cup light brown sugar

½ cup chopped walnuts

½ teaspoon ground cinnamon

Preparation

1 Preheat oven to 350 degrees F. Coat a 9- x 13-inch baking dish with cooking spray.

2 In a large bowl with an electric mixer, beat cake mix, the 6 tablespoons melted butter, and 1 cup oats; mix until crumbly. Reserve ¾ cup mixture and set aside. Add eggs to remaining crumb mixture and beat until well combined; press into baking dish to create the bottom crust. Pour pie filling evenly over batter.

3 In a medium bowl, combine reserved crumb mixture, the remaining ¼ cup oats, the 2 tablespoons softened butter, the brown sugar, walnuts, and cinnamon; mix well. Sprinkle mixture evenly over filling.

4 Bake 35 to 40 minutes, or until golden and cake is set. Let cool before cutting into squares.

Fancy It Up: *To give this a fresh-from-the-patch look, garnish each piece with a few fresh blueberries.*

Farmhouse Butterscotch Blondies

We got the idea for these butterscotch beauties from an old farmhouse cookbook that dates back to the beginning of the century. While we changed them up to make them a lot simpler, we made sure to keep the old-fashioned flavor that has made them a timeless favorite. Oh, and we found it was a lot more convenient to bake these in a traditional oven rather than in an open hearth.

Makes 15

Ingredients

1 package golden butter cake mix

1 stick (½ cup) butter, melted

2 eggs

¼ cup water

1 teaspoon vanilla extract

½ cup butterscotch chips

½ cup chopped walnuts

Preparation

1 Preheat oven to 325 degrees F. Coat an 8-inch square baking dish with cooking spray.

2 In a large bowl with an electric mixer, beat cake mix, butter, eggs, water, and vanilla until thoroughly combined. Stir in butterscotch chips and walnuts. Pour batter into baking dish.

3 Bake 30 to 35 minutes, or until a toothpick inserted in center comes out clean. Let cool completely, then cut.

Test Kitchen Tip: *If your market doesn't carry the golden butter cake mix, then you can just use a yellow cake mix. Rest assured, your bars will still be just as tasty and there'll be lots of butterscotch flavor in every bite.*

Spirited Irish Cream Cake

While taping a series of shows in Ireland a few years ago, we fell in love with the landscape, the people, and their "spirits". No, we're not talking about everyone's cheerful disposition; we're talking about their famous cordials, whiskey, and beer. Inspired by the good times we had, we decided to whip up this spirited dessert. You're going to love the velvety goodness that the Irish cream liqueur adds to this super moist and flavorful cake.

Serves 15

Ingredients

1 package white cake mix

3 eggs

½ cup vegetable oil

½ cup water

1 teaspoon vanilla extract

¾ cup Irish cream liqueur, divided

1 (4-ounce) package white chocolate baking bar, for garnish

FROSTING

1-½ sticks (¾ cup) butter

¼ cup cocoa powder

¼ cup Irish cream liqueur

4 cups confectioners' sugar

Preparation

1 Preheat oven to 325 degrees F. Coat a 9- x 13-inch baking dish with cooking spray.

2 In a large bowl with an electric mixer, beat cake mix, eggs, oil, water, vanilla, and ½ cup liqueur until thoroughly combined. Pour batter into baking dish.

3 Bake 30 to 35 minutes, or until a toothpick inserted in center comes out clean. Let cool 10 minutes, then prick holes in top of cake with a fork. Pour ¼ cup liqueur evenly over cake. Let cool completely.

4 To make frosting, in a large bowl with an electric mixer, beat butter, cocoa powder, and ¼ cup liqueur until creamy. Slowly add confectioners' sugar, beating until smooth. Evenly spread over top of cake. Using a potato peeler, shave white baking bar, lengthwise, to make curls; gently place on top of cake. Keep refrigerated.

Test Kitchen Tip: *Whenever you make chocolate curls, make sure the bar is at room temperature and not refrigerated; this way, you'll get longer curls. Also, shave them over a plate so they don't go all over the place. And the best way to pick these up is with a toothpick, since the warmth of your hands can cause the chocolate to melt.*

HOLIDAY SPECIAL

Orange Grove Butter Bars

Missourians will tell you, you haven't lived until you've tried gooey butter cake, and they're right, it's absolutely delicious. But, we wanted more. So, we decided to put a California spin on them. By adding just a little bit of orange zest and taking some convenient shortcuts, we've come up with our own citrusy-delicious version that's ooey-gooey-yummy. You may not be able to stop at just one bar.

Serves 16

Ingredients

1 package yellow cake mix

1-½ sticks (¾ cup) butter, melted, divided

3 eggs, divided

1 (8-ounce) package cream cheese, softened

1 teaspoon vanilla extract

Zest of 1 orange

1 (16-ounce) package confectioners' sugar

Preparation

1 Preheat oven to 350 degrees F. Coat a 9- x 13-inch baking dish with cooking spray.

2 In a large bowl with an electric mixer, beat cake mix, 1 stick butter, and 1 egg until thoroughly combined. Lightly press mixture into baking dish.

3 In a medium bowl, beat cream cheese, the remaining 2 eggs, the vanilla, orange zest, and remaining ½ stick butter. Slowly beat in confectioners' sugar until thoroughly combined. Spread mixture over batter.

4 Bake 45 to 50 minutes, or until the top is golden. Be careful not to overbake; center should be slightly gooey. When cool, slice into bars and serve. Keep refrigerated.

Chocolate Raspberry Dream Cake

Pairing chocolate and raspberries together is certainly nothing new. Some people will add a layer of raspberry preserves to a cake or sprinkle a few fresh berries on top and call it a day. But we like to go all out, so we actually baked all of the berry-liciousness right into the cake itself, which makes it burst with flavor. That, and some dollops of our sour cream topping, and it's no wonder why this cake tastes like a dream.

Serves 15

Ingredients

1 package devil's food cake mix

1 (21-ounce) can raspberry pie filling

4 eggs

½ cup mini chocolate chips

TOPPING

1 (4-serving size) package instant vanilla pudding mix

2 cups sour cream

½ cup milk

1 teaspoon vanilla extract

Preparation

1   Preheat oven to 350 degrees F. Coat a 9- x 13-inch baking dish with cooking spray.

2   In a large bowl with an electric mixer, beat cake mix, pie filling, and eggs until thoroughly combined. Stir in chocolate chips. Pour batter evenly into baking dish. Bake 35 to 40 minutes, or until a toothpick inserted in center comes out clean. Let cool.

3   To make topping, in a medium bowl, whisk pudding mix, sour cream, milk, and vanilla until smooth and creamy. When ready to serve, dollop over cake. Keep refrigerated.

Finishing Touch: *As you can see, a fresh raspberry and some mint really add a "wow" factor.*

Lunch Box PB&J Bars

If you grew up eating peanut butter and jelly sandwiches and still love them today, then get ready for a treat that'll make you feel like a kid all over again. These simple bars are just as perfect for tucking into your lunch box as they are for setting out on Bunco night. Just serve with a glass of milk and enjoy taking a trip down memory lane.

Serves 14

Ingredients

1 package white cake mix

2 eggs

⅓ cup vegetable oil

½ cup peanut butter

1 teaspoon vanilla extract

½ cup grape jelly

1 cup peanut butter chips

Preparation

1 Preheat oven to 350 degrees F. Coat a 9- x 13-inch baking dish with cooking spray.

2 In a large bowl with an electric mixer, beat cake mix, eggs, oil, peanut butter, and vanilla until thoroughly combined. Set aside ½ cup of dough for topping. Press remaining dough into baking dish. Spread jelly over dough.

3 In a small bowl, combine peanut butter chips with reserved ½ cup dough until crumbly. Sprinkle crumbles evenly over jelly.

4 Bake 25 to 30 minutes, or until golden. Allow to cool before cutting.

So Many Options: *Feel free to use your favorite flavor of jam or jelly in these bars. Maybe one week you can make them with strawberry and the next with grape?*

Chocolate Hazelnut Crumb Cake

There's a reason why people buy jars and jars of a certain popular chocolate hazelnut spread. It's addictive! And if you're like some of us in the Test Kitchen (we won't mention who...), you've probably found yourself with just a jar and a spoon on many an occasion. Luckily, we've come up with an even better way for you to enjoy your favorite spread, and we're sharing it below. There's a pretty good chance that this'll become your new go-to favorite.

Serves 14

Ingredients

1 package yellow cake mix

1 stick (½ cup) butter, softened

1 egg

2 teaspoons vanilla extract

¾ cup oats

1 (13-ounce jar) chocolate-hazelnut spread

Preparation

1 Preheat oven to 350 degrees F. Coat a 7- x 11-inch baking dish with cooking spray.

2 In a large bowl with an electric mixer, beat cake mix, butter, egg, and vanilla until thoroughly combined. Add oats and mix well. (Dough will be stiff.)

3 Press half the dough into the bottom of baking dish. Gently spread the chocolate-hazelnut spread on top of dough. Crumble remaining dough over the chocolate.

4 Bake 25 to 30 minutes, or until golden around the edges. Let cool before cutting into bars.

Orange Pineapple Angel Cake

Picture yourself sitting by the pool, basking in the sun, and sipping something cool and refreshing. You're craving dessert, but you want to keep it light. What do you go for? If the picture on the opposite page just caught your attention, then you're right on track. This cake, full of the tropical flavors of orange and pineapple, is summertime perfect. We suggest making it ahead of time, so it's ready when you are.

Serves 15

Ingredients

1 package angel food cake mix, prepared according to package directions for a tube pan

1 (4-serving size) package sugar-free orange gelatin mix

¾ cup boiling water

½ cup cold water

1 (4-serving size) package sugar-free instant vanilla pudding mix

1-½ cups fat-free milk

1 (8-ounce) can crushed pineapple, drained well

2 teaspoons orange zest

1 (8-ounce) container fat-free frozen whipped topping, thawed

Preparation

1 Cut the baked and cooled angel food cake into 12 slices and place each slice on its side in a 9- x 13-inch baking dish, slightly overlapping if necessary.

2 In a medium bowl, dissolve gelatin mix in boiling water, then stir in cold water. Slowly pour over cake; refrigerate 1 hour.

3 In a large bowl, whisk vanilla pudding mix and milk until thickened. Stir in pineapple, orange zest, and whipped topping. Evenly spread over cake. Cover and refrigerate 1 hour, or until ready to serve. Keep refrigerated.

Fancy It Up: Sure, you can serve this as-is, but for special occasions you might want to garnish each slice with an orange wedge and a couple of pineapple chunks. It's simple, but it really dresses it up!

LIGHTER OPTION

Roadside Strawberries Shortcake Stacks

We were taught at an early age that when life gives us lemons, we need to make lemonade. And from that, we also learned that when our markets and roadside stands have strawberries at rock-bottom prices, we need to find creative ways to use them. That's why we decided to make a basic shortcake something special by making it extra moist and adding homemade whipped cream and lots of fresh berries.

Serves 9

Ingredients

1 package white cake mix

½ cup sour cream

1 cup water

⅓ cup vegetable oil

3 egg whites

2 cups heavy cream

1 teaspoon vanilla extract

½ cup confectioners' sugar

1 pound strawberries, divided

Strawberry ice cream topping for drizzling

Preparation

1 Preheat oven to 350 degrees F. Coat a 10- x 15-inch rimmed baking sheet with cooking spray.

2 In a large bowl with an electric mixer, beat cake mix, sour cream, water, oil, and egg whites until thoroughly combined. Pour batter onto baking sheet. Bake 15 to 20 minutes, or until a toothpick inserted in center comes out clean. Let cool completely.

3 In a large bowl with an electric mixer, beat heavy cream, vanilla, and confectioners' sugar until stiff peaks form. Set 8 strawberries aside for garnish, and slice the remaining berries.

4 Cut cake into 18 equal-size pieces. Place a piece of cake on a plate, pile with whipped cream and top with sliced strawberries. Top with another piece of cake, finish with more whipped cream, and garnish with a whole strawberry. Repeat until all cake pieces are used. Before serving, drizzle with strawberry topping.

Brownie Bonanza

Chewy Chocolaty Caramel Coconut Brownies

One bite and you'll be saying, "Give me some more!" At least that's what we all said when they first came out of the Test Kitchen. In fact, we may have tested these just a few more times than necessary...just to be extra-certain that they were perfect (they are!). You just can't beat these caramel and coconut-topped chocolaty brownies; they're sinfully tasty!

Makes 18

Ingredients

2 cups sweetened shredded coconut

1 package brownie mix, batter prepared according to package directions

1 (11-ounce) package caramels

¼ cup heavy cream

1 cup semi-sweet chocolate chips

1 teaspoon vegetable shortening

Preparation

1 To toast coconut, spread evenly on a rimmed baking sheet. Bake at 375 degrees F for 8 to 10 minutes, or until golden brown; set aside. (The coconut will brown quickly so keep an eye on it.)

2 Reduce oven temperature to bake brownies according to package directions for a 9- x 13-inch baking dish.

3 In a saucepan over low heat, combine caramels and heavy cream and cook until caramels are melted and smooth, stirring constantly. Add toasted coconut to caramel mixture; mix well. Evenly spread coconut mixture over brownies.

4 In a microwave-safe bowl, combine chocolate chips and shortening; microwave 60 to 75 seconds, or until chocolate chips are melted and smooth, stirring occasionally. Drizzle or pipe chocolate over brownies. Refrigerate 15 minutes, or until chocolate has hardened. Cut into squares.

Double Mint Brownie Sundaes

From the mint chocolate pieces that we've put into the batter to the mint chip ice cream that's layered on top, you can count on lots of minty goodness in this mouthwatering brownie sundae. And when you add a drizzle of hot fudge, it's even better. This dessert wins the prize for double-mint delicious and everyday easy. So, don't tease your taste buds any longer and let's get started!

Makes 12

Ingredients

1 (4.67-ounce) package crème de menthe thin mint candies, chopped, divided

1 package brownie mix, batter prepared according to package directions

1 quart mint chocolate chip ice cream, slightly softened

1 (12-ounce) jar hot fudge ice cream topping, warmed

Preparation

1 Preheat oven to 350 degrees F. Coat an 8-inch square baking dish with cooking spray.

2 Stir half the mint candies into the brownie batter, then pour into baking dish. Bake 35 to 40 minutes, or until a toothpick inserted in center comes out clean; let cool completely.

3 Firmly pack the ice cream evenly over brownies. Freeze at least 4 hours, or until firm. When ready to serve, cut into squares, drizzle with hot fudge and sprinkle with remaining mint candies. Keep frozen.

So Many Options: *If you want to take these over the top, you can always sprinkle the baked brownies with about a 1/4 cup of crème de menthe liqueur before topping with ice cream.*

FROZEN TREAT

Peanut Butter Pretzel Brownies

This is the sweet and salty dessert you've been dreaming about all day long. After all, it's made with a rich and fudgy brownie batter that's studded with lots of chocolate chips and swirled with your favorite kind of peanut butter. Then, to take it over the top, we sprinkle on pretzel pieces before baking it off. Mmm...isn't it time you made your dream come true?

Serves 9

Ingredients

½ cup semi-sweet chocolate chips

1 package brownie mix, batter prepared according to package directions

½ cup creamy peanut butter

¾ cup coarsely crushed pretzels

Preparation

1 Preheat oven to 350 degrees F. Coat an 8-inch square baking dish with cooking spray.

2 Stir chocolate chips into prepared batter; pour into baking dish.

3 Place peanut butter in a microwave-safe bowl; microwave 10 to 15 seconds, or until pourable. Drizzle over brownie batter and swirl with a knife. Sprinkle pretzels over batter, then lightly press into batter.

4 Bake 45 minutes, or until a toothpick inserted in center comes out clean. Let cool, then cut into squares.

Test Kitchen Tip: *If you crave a nuttier, crunchier brownie, use chunky peanut butter instead of creamy.*

Crowd Pleasin' Black Forest Trifle

Black Forest Cake is a multi-layered German cake that features lots of chocolate, cherries, and whipped cream. While we weren't looking to reinvent the wheel, we did want to come up with an easier way for you to share the goodness with your crowd. That's why we came up with this elegant-looking, but super simple, trifle version. It comes together in no time and tastes like pure decadence!

Serves 16

Ingredients

1 cup dark chocolate chips

1 package brownie mix, batter prepared according to package directions

1 (6-serving size) package vanilla pudding mix

3 cups milk

1 (21-ounce) can cherry pie filling

1 (16-ounce) container frozen whipped topping, thawed

Shaved chocolate for garnish

Preparation

1 Preheat oven to 350 degrees F. Coat a 9- x 13-inch baking dish with cooking spray. Stir chocolate chips into prepared brownie batter; spread evenly in baking dish.

2 Bake 25 to 30 minutes, or until a toothpick inserted in center comes out clean; let cool.

3 In a large bowl, whisk pudding mix and milk until slightly thickened.

4 Break up brownies into 2-inch pieces and place half in the bottom of a trifle bowl or large glass serving bowl. Cover with half the pudding mixture, half the pie filling, and half the whipped topping. Repeat layers, then garnish with chocolate curls. Cover and chill at least 2 hours before serving. Keep refrigerated.

Note: To learn how to curl chocolate see page 148.

Did You Know? *Dark chocolate chips have a super-rich flavor that's even more intense than semi-sweet chocolate chips. In this recipe, they add a deep, chocolaty taste to your trifle. You can easily find these in the baking aisle of your market with all the other chocolate chip varieties.*

Sweet Heat Mexican Brownies

Before you take a look at the ingredients and start thinking that something must be wrong with this recipe, we want to assure you that what you're seeing is absolutely right. We have purposefully added a bit of hot pepper to these brownies. The pepper helps to sharpen the taste of the chocolate and, when combined with the cinnamon, adds a tasty south-of-the-border flavor. We hope you'll let curiosity take hold, because you're going to love this unique combination!

Makes 15

Ingredients

1 package brownie mix

²/₃ cup vegetable oil

¼ cup water

2 eggs

1 teaspoon ground cinnamon

½ teaspoon cayenne pepper

¼ teaspoon salt

1 (4.25-ounce) dark chocolate candy bar, chopped

Preparation

1 Preheat oven to 350 degrees F. Coat a 9- x 13-inch baking dish with cooking spray.

2 In a large bowl, combine brownie mix, oil, water, and eggs; mix well. Stir in cinnamon, cayenne pepper, salt, and dark chocolate. Spread batter evenly into baking dish.

3 Bake 25 to 30 minutes, or until a toothpick inserted in center comes out clean. Let cool, then cut into squares.

Frozen Espresso Brownie Bowl

You drink it every morning. You have a cup as a pick-me-up in the afternoon. Heck, you even enjoy it as a treat after dinner. It's true, you're a bonafide coffee lover. And for you, our coffee-loving friend, we've come up with this frozen dessert that's made with...oh yeah, coffee liqueur AND coffee-flavored ice cream. Now you've got to make the big decision about whether or not you're going to share.

Serves 10

Ingredients

1 package brownie mix, batter prepared according to package directions

¼ cup coffee liqueur

1 quart mocha chip ice cream, softened

1 (8-ounce) container frozen whipped topping, thawed

¼ cup crushed chocolate-covered espresso beans (optional)

Preparation

1 Preheat oven to 350 degrees F. Bake brownies according to package directions for a 9- x 13-inch baking dish; let cool. Pour liqueur over brownies, let absorb. Cut into squares.

2 Meanwhile, line an approximately 2-½-quart bowl with plastic wrap. Place about 2/3 of brownies into bowl; press brownies together, molding them to the bowl, up to about an inch from the top. Spoon the ice cream into bowl, pressing firmly so it is well packed. Place remaining brownies over top and press firmly into ice cream. Cover with plastic wrap and freeze overnight.

3 When ready to serve, remove top layer of plastic wrap and invert bowl onto a serving platter. Remove bowl, then remaining plastic wrap. Spread whipped topping evenly over brownie bowl. Sprinkle with espresso beans, if desired. Keep frozen.

Finishing Touch: *Although chocolate-covered espresso beans are very popular and can be found in most markets, if you can't find them you can trim off some of the crispy brownie edges to grate over the top.*

FROZEN TREAT

Buckeye Brownies

Who would've thought that the nut of the Ohio buckeye tree would become the inspiration for one of the most popular confections of all time? A buckeye cookie (or candy, depending on where you're from) is basically a peanut butter fudge ball that's dipped in chocolate to resemble the tree nut. And if you've ever had the pleasure of trying them, you know exactly why they're loved. Our brownie version is even more special-tasting and so much easier.

Makes 16

Ingredients

1 package gluten-free brownie mix, batter prepared according to package directions (see Tip)

1 cup creamy peanut butter

1 stick (½ cup) butter, softened

2 tablespoons milk

1 teaspoon vanilla extract

2 cups confectioners' sugar

1-½ cups milk chocolate chips

3 tablespoons vegetable shortening

Preparation

1 Preheat oven to 350 degrees F. Bake brownies according to package directions for an 8-inch baking dish; let cool.

2 In a large bowl with an electric mixer, beat peanut butter and butter until creamy. Add milk, vanilla, and confectioners' sugar; beat until thoroughly combined. Evenly spread mixture over brownies.

3 In a small saucepan over low heat, melt chocolate chips and shortening until smooth, stirring constantly. Evenly spread over peanut butter mixture. After the chocolate hardens, cut into squares.

Test Kitchen Tip: *We tested this with gluten-free and traditional brownie mixes and both yielded amazing results! If you're concerned about gluten in your diet, as always, please make sure that all the ingredients you are using for this recipe are labeled gluten-free.*

GLUTEN FREE

Chocolate Cherry Cheesecake Brownies

You could add a cheesecake swirl to anything and it would make it instantly better, but we wanted to go for a little more with these brownies, so we scheduled an impromptu brainstorming session with everyone in the Test Kitchen. After a long deliberation, it was finally decided that chocolate, cherries, and cheesecake would make the ultimate winning combination. We think we made the right decision, but we'll let you be the judge.

Makes 12

Ingredients

½ cup dried cherries

½ cup chocolate chips

1 package brownie mix, batter prepared according to package directions

1 (8-ounce) package cream cheese, softened

1 egg

1 teaspoon vanilla extract

Preparation

1 Preheat oven to 350 degrees F. Coat an 8-inch square baking dish with cooking spray.

2 Stir cherries and chocolate chips into prepared brownie batter and spread evenly in baking dish.

3 In a bowl with an electric mixer, combine cream cheese, egg, and vanilla until fluffy. Dollop cream cheese mixture over batter. Using a butter knife, swirl the cream cheese mixture through the batter.

4 Bake 40 to 45 minutes, or until a toothpick inserted in center comes out clean. Let cool completely, then cut and serve. Keep refrigerated.

Did You Know? *The reason we don't list the package sizes for our brownie and cake mixes is because this varies from manufacturer to manufacturer. We've tested our recipes with many different national brands and have found that our recipes work with just about all of them.*

Powder Puff Brownie Balls

Life is complicated enough without having to make tough decisions at the dessert table. That's the reason why we like to roll half of these fudgy brownie balls in powdered sugar and the other half in cocoa powder. It makes it easy for us to try one of each or two of our favorite kind. And if you set these out for a party, your guests will appreciate having a couple of options.

Makes 28

Ingredients

1 package brownie mix

⅔ cup vegetable oil

¼ cup strong brewed coffee

2 eggs

½ cup chopped walnuts

¼ cup confectioners' sugar

¼ cup cocoa powder

Preparation

1 Preheat oven to 350 degrees F. Coat a 9- x 13-inch baking dish with cooking spray.

2 In a large bowl, combine brownie mix, oil, coffee, and eggs; mix well. Stir in walnuts. Spread mixture evenly in baking dish.

3 Bake 20 to 25 minutes, or until a toothpick inserted in center comes out clean. (Do not overbake.) Let cool 20 minutes. While still slightly warm, using a small ice cream scoop or soup spoon, scoop out enough to roll into 1-inch balls. Place on baking sheet; let cool completely.

4 Place confectioners' sugar and cocoa powder into two separate bowls. Roll half the brownie balls in confectioners' sugar and the other half in cocoa powder. Place in an airtight container until ready to serve.

Serving Suggestion: *We like to place each brownie ball into a mini cupcake liner for serving. This way you and your guests won't get powdered sugar or cocoa all over your fingers. Plus, you can use festive liners to go with your party's theme!*

Slow Cooker S'mores Pudding

Now you can enjoy the taste of your favorite outdoor treat with the convenience of dump, layer, and dig in. Honestly, it's that easy! And since it's made in your slow cooker, you can set it to start cooking just a few hours before your family movie night or game night begins, so that it's ready when you are.

Serves 8

Ingredients

1 package brownie mix, batter prepared according to package directions

1 (4-serving size) package instant chocolate pudding mix

2 cups milk

1 cup coarsely crushed graham crackers

1 cup mini marshmallows

Preparation

1 Coat a 5-quart or larger slow cooker with cooking spray. Pour prepared brownie batter into slow cooker.

2 In a medium bowl, whisk pudding mix and milk until slightly thickened. Pour slowly over brownie batter. Sprinkle graham crackers on top.

3 Cover and cook on HIGH 2 to 2-½ hours, or until edges are done. Center will be slightly wet. Sprinkle with marshmallows, cover, and continue to cook until marshmallows are melted. Serve warm.

Serving Suggestion: *There are lots of different ways to enjoy this dessert. Some of us in the Test Kitchen preferred it as-is, while others liked it with ice cream or a dollop of whipped cream. No matter how you serve it, it's sure to deliver lots of "OOH IT'S SO GOOD!!®"*

SLOW COOKER

Cookie Crazy

4-Ingredient
Candy Bar Cookies

Typically, when it's time to make cookies, you've got to bring out the canisters of sugar and flour, along with the baking soda, butter, eggs, and flavorings. That's not to mention the bowls for mixing dry and wet ingredients, the measuring cups, the spoons...are you exhausted yet? For your everyday cookie cravings we came up with this melts-in-your-mouth cookie recipe that's made with just 4 ingredients. Easy never tasted so good!

Makes 36 cookies

Ingredients

1 package white cake mix

⅓ cup vegetable oil

2 eggs

1-½ cups chopped candy bars (see note)

Preparation

1 Preheat oven to 350 degrees F. Coat baking sheets with cooking spray.

2 In a large bowl with an electric mixer, beat cake mix, oil, and eggs until thoroughly combined. Stir in candy bar pieces. Drop by teaspoonfuls 2 inches apart onto baking sheets.

3 Bake 7 to 10 minutes, or until golden. Cool on wire racks, then store in an airtight container.

Mix 'n' Match: *You can mix and match almost any of your favorite candy bars in this recipe! However, we think these cookies are truly best when made with candy bars that have a nutty, gooey filling.*

Carrot Cake Cookies with Cream Cheese Frosting

Good news! You no longer have to bake a whole cake to enjoy a taste of that carrot cake you've been craving all day. Instead, you can just make these super easy and super tasty cookies, which can be ready in under 30 minutes. Oh, and did we mention they're topped with a homemade cream cheese frosting? It's a good thing this recipe makes a big batch, because these are going to disappear!

Makes 36 cookies

Ingredients

1 package carrot cake mix

1 (8-ounce) can crushed pineapple, drained

2 carrots, finely shredded

2 eggs

2 tablespoons vegetable oil

1 cup chopped pecans

FROSTING

1 (8-ounce) package cream cheese, softened

1 stick (½ cup) butter, softened

2 cups confectioners' sugar

Preparation

1 Preheat oven to 350 degrees F. Coat baking sheets with cooking spray.

2 In a large bowl with an electric mixer, beat cake mix, pineapple, carrots, eggs, and oil until thoroughly combined; stir in pecans. Drop by teaspoonfuls, 1 inch apart on baking sheets.

3 Bake 14 to 16 minutes, or until edges are golden. Remove to a wire rack to cool completely.

4 To make frosting, in a medium bowl with an electric mixer, beat cream cheese and butter until creamy. Slowly add confectioners' sugar and beat until smooth. Frost cookies, then store in an airtight container.

Test Kitchen Tips: *If you're really pressed for time, you could use a canned cream cheese frosting instead of our homemade one, but you may not want to take that shortcut once you've tasted ours! And for an extra-special touch, we suggest sprinkling some shredded carrots over the frosting.*

Chocolate-Drizzled Almond Macaroons

We can't help it - we love ourselves a good macaroon, and this is one heck of a good macaroon. Crispy edges of toasted coconut, super moist centers, and a chocolate drizzle make it hard to resist having one after another. And hey, doesn't this combination remind you of a popular candy bar that's full of "joy"? Oh yeah, we think of everything!

Makes 24 cookies

Ingredients

1 package angel food cake mix

½ cup cold water

1 teaspoon almond extract

1 (14-ounce) bag (about 5 cups) sweetened coconut

½ cup slivered almonds, minced

½ cup semisweet chocolate chips

1 teaspoon shortening

Preparation

1 Preheat oven to 325 degrees F. Line 2 baking sheets with parchment paper.

2 In a large bowl with an electric mixer, beat cake mix, water, and almond extract until thoroughly combined. Add coconut and almonds; mix well. Scoop 2 tablespoons at a time and drop onto baking sheets about 2 inches apart.

3 Bake 20 to 22 minutes, or until lightly browned. Cool 5 minutes, then remove to a wire rack to cool completely.

4 In a small microwave-safe bowl, melt chocolate chips and shortening 60 to 75 seconds, stirring occasionally until smooth. Using the tines of a fork, drizzle the melted chocolate over the macaroons and let sit until chocolate is firm. Store in an airtight container.

Just-for-Art Butter Pecan Cookies

Did you know that Art Ginsburg ("Mr. Food") loved anything that was butter pecan flavored? Butter pecan was always his first choice when it came to ice cream, decadent fudge, and...you guessed it, cookies. So, as a "thank you" to the man who founded our great company, we made sure to include a cookie recipe that features his love of this nutty combination.

Makes 30 cookies

Ingredients

¼ cup sugar

1 teaspoon ground cinnamon

1 package butter pecan cake mix

⅓ cup butter, melted

2 eggs

½ cup chopped pecans

30 pecan halves for garnish

Preparation

1 Preheat oven to 350 degrees F. In a shallow dish, combine sugar and cinnamon; mix well and set aside.

2 In a large bowl with an electric mixer, beat cake mix, butter, and eggs until thoroughly combined. Stir in chopped pecans.

3 Form dough into 1-inch balls, then roll in sugar mixture until evenly coated. Place on ungreased baking sheets, about 2 inches apart. Place a pecan half in the center of each ball and press in slightly.

4 Bake 9 to 12 minutes, or until golden. Let cool 5 minutes, then remove to a wire rack to cool completely. Store in an airtight container.

Did You Know? *According to the National Pecan Shellers Association, Albany, GA has more than 600,000 pecan trees, which is probably why it was nicknamed "the pecan capital of the U.S." The city also hosts the annual National Pecan Festival, which includes a race, parade, cooking contests, the crowning of the National Pecan Queen, and more!*

Chocolate Cream Cookie Cups

Okay, we're going to ask you to close your eyes. No, not now, or you won't be able to read the rest of the recipe, but just before you sink your teeth into one of these Chocolate Cream Cookie Cups. Then, once you've had one (or two, or three), you've got to let us know what you think. Don't be surprised if you end up discovering that they're every bit as good as the best chocolate cream pie you've ever tasted.

Makes 28 cookie cups

Ingredients

1 (17.5-ounce) package sugar cookie mix

1 stick (½ cup) butter, melted

1 egg

1 (4-serving size) package cook and serve chocolate pudding mix

1 cup whipped topping

1 small chocolate bar, grated

Preparation

1 Preheat oven to 350 degrees F. Coat 28 mini muffin cups with cooking spray.

2 In a large bowl with an electric mixer, beat cookie mix, butter, and egg until thoroughly combined. Roll dough into 1-inch balls and place in muffin cups. Using your thumb, press dough into each cup, forming a crust and leaving an indentation in the center.

3 Bake 15 to 18 minutes, or until golden. Remove from oven and, using the handle of a wooden spoon, gently press into center of each cookie to make a 1-inch indentation. Let cool 5 minutes, then remove to a wire rack to cool completely.

4 Meanwhile, in a saucepan, prepare pudding according to package directions. Fill each cookie cup evenly with pudding. Refrigerate 15 minutes. Top each filled cookie cup with a dollop of whipped topping and a sprinkle of grated chocolate. Keep refrigerated.

Test Kitchen Tip: *The best time to grate a chocolate bar is when it's at room temperature. If it's too cold, it will crumble and if it's too warm, you'll end up with a sticky mess.*

Lemon Cheesecake Crinkle Cookies

Lemon desserts are a springtime favorite, and these lemony cookies are sure to add lots of sweet sunshine to your days. The cream cheese and butter give them a velvety smooth texture, while the lemon cake mix and fresh lemon zest add just the right amount of zing. The results are so dreamy, you may want to gift a few to your favorite people!

Makes 36 cookies

Ingredients

1 (8-ounce) package cream cheese, softened

½ stick (¼ cup) butter, softened

1 package lemon cake mix

1 egg

¼ teaspoon vanilla extract

1 teaspoon lemon zest

½ cup confectioners' sugar

Preparation

1 Preheat oven to 375 degrees F.

2 In a large bowl with an electric mixer, beat cream cheese and butter until creamy. Add cake mix, egg, vanilla, and lemon zest; beat until thoroughly combined.

3 Shape dough into 1-inch balls; roll in confectioners' sugar to coat. Place on ungreased baking sheets, about 1 inch apart.

4 Bake 10 to 12 minutes, or until light golden around edges. Let cool 5 minutes, then remove to wire racks to cool completely. Store in an airtight container.

Test Kitchen Tip: *When zesting a lemon, make sure you use the bright yellow skin, which contains all the fresh-tasting oils, rather than the white pithy layer underneath it, which tends to be bitter.*

Crisscross Peanut Butter Cookies

You only need to set aside 20 minutes to whip up a batch of these semi-homemade, extra-nutty, peanut butter cookies. They're exactly what all peanut butter cookies should be like. We even took care to mark them with the signature crisscross pattern, so there's no mistaking these for other cookie jar favorites. We're always looking out for you!

Makes 32 cookies

Ingredients

1 package yellow cake mix

1 cup creamy peanut butter

⅓ cup vegetable oil

2 eggs

1 teaspoon vanilla extract

¼ cup peanuts, chopped

Preparation

1 Preheat oven to 350 degrees F.

2 In a large bowl with an electric mixer, beat cake mix, peanut butter, oil, eggs, and vanilla until thoroughly combined.

3 Roll dough into 1-inch balls and place on ungreased baking sheets, about 2 inches apart. Using a fork, flatten gently in a crisscross pattern. Sprinkle with peanuts.

4 Bake 10 to 12 minutes, or until light golden around edges. Remove to wire racks to cool completely. Store in an airtight container.

Drunken Walnut Fudge Cookies

These cookies aren't for little ones being tucked into bed at night. These are the cookies you make when you're having an adults-only occasion. That's because every bite is studded with lots of rum-soaked walnuts, and each cookie is drizzled with a homemade chocolate rum glaze. It's just enough to make them a little "tipsy" (we mean that in a fun and flavorful way, of course!).

Makes 28 cookies

Ingredients

¾ cup coarsely chopped walnuts

¼ cup rum

1 package chocolate cake mix

¼ cup vegetable oil

1 egg

GLAZE

1 cup confectioners' sugar

2 tablespoons cocoa powder

2 tablespoons rum

1 teaspoon water

Preparation

1 Preheat oven to 350 degrees F. Coat baking sheets with cooking spray. In a small bowl, combine walnuts and the ¼ cup rum; let soak 10 minutes.

2 In a large bowl with an electric mixer, beat cake mix, oil, egg, and the soaked walnuts until thoroughly combined. Drop by tablespoonfuls, about 2 inches apart, onto baking sheets.

3 Bake 10 to 12 minutes, or until edges are firm. Cool 5 minutes, then remove to wire racks to cool completely.

4 To make glaze, in a medium bowl, combine sugar and cocoa powder; whisk in 2 tablespoons rum and water until smooth. Drizzle over cooled cookies and let set until glaze is hardened. Store in an airtight container.

Fourth of July Cookies

These are the perfect, easy cookies to make and take to this year's Fourth of July bash, or anytime you want to show off your American spirit. Speckled with candy-coated chocolate pieces in red, white, and blue, they're a fun treat that everyone will enjoy. We suggest bringing these out on a big platter with a pitcher of icy lemonade to wash them down, maybe just before the big fireworks show.

Makes 24 cookies

Ingredients

1 package white cake mix

2 eggs

⅓ cup vegetable oil

¾ cup red and blue candy-coated chocolates

¾ cup white baking chips

Preparation

1 Preheat oven to 350 degrees F. Coat baking sheets with cooking spray.

2 In a large bowl with an electric mixer, beat cake mix, eggs, and oil until thoroughly combined. Stir in candy and baking chips. Drop by teaspoonfuls onto baking sheets, about 2 inches apart.

3 Bake 8 to 10 minutes, or until the edges are light golden. Remove to wire racks to cool completely. Store in an airtight container.

So Many Options: *While we went for a patriotic theme with these cookies, you can make them to fit any other theme you like just by switching up the color of your candy-coated chocolates. For example, you might want to bake these up for a baby shower using pastel-colored chocolates or at Christmastime with red and green chocolates. The choice is up to you!*

HOLIDAY SPECIAL

Choco-Mint Sandwich Cookies

Are you tired of counting down the days until the Girl Scouts release your favorite thin, chocolate-mint cookies? Now, you no longer have to! We took everything you love about their best-selling cookie and doubled the goodness to make our own inspired recipe. How can you top fresh-tasting mint filling, sandwiched between two chocolate cookies, and dipped in dark chocolate? You can't! This one may just earn you a "best baker" badge.

Makes 24 sandwich cookies

Ingredients

1 package chocolate cake mix

⅓ cup vegetable oil

2 eggs

¼ cup water

½ stick (¼-cup) butter, softened

2 ounces cream cheese, softened

2 cups confectioners' sugar

1 teaspoon mint extract

2 to 3 drops green food color

1 (12-ounce) package dark chocolate chips

2 teaspoons vegetable shortening

Preparation

1 Preheat oven to 375 degrees F.

2 In a large bowl with an electric mixer, beat cake mix, oil, eggs, and water until thoroughly combined. Drop 48 teaspoonfuls of batter onto ungreased baking sheets, about 2 inches apart. Bake 8 to 10 minutes, or until cookies are set. Remove to wire racks to cool completely.

3 Meanwhile, in a medium bowl with an electric mixer, beat butter and cream cheese until creamy. Add confectioners' sugar, mint extract, and food color, and beat until fluffy. Place a teaspoon of filling in center of one chocolate cookie and gently press another cookie on top, until cream comes to the edge. Repeat with remaining cookies.

4 In a small microwave-safe bowl, combine chocolate chips and shortening. Microwave 60 to 75 seconds, stirring occasionally until smooth,. Dip about ⅓ of each sandwich cookie into chocolate glaze, and place on wax paper. Repeat with remaining cookies. Refrigerate until chocolate is set. Keep refrigerated.

Did You Know? *Using shortening in the chocolate glaze gives it a nice shine when it firms up.*

Super Simple Snickerdoodles

We hope we didn't twist your tongue too much with the name of these cookies! To make it up to you, we've made sure these snickerdoodles are as simple to make as possible. Much softer and lighter than traditional sugar cookies, our snickerdoodles make a great after-school, after-work, or after-anytime treat. You're going to love their cinnamon-kissed taste!

Makes 24 cookies

Ingredients

1 package yellow cake mix

⅓ cup vegetable oil

2 eggs

2 teaspoons vanilla extract

1/3 cup sugar

1-½ teaspoons ground cinnamon

Preparation

1 Preheat oven to 350 degrees F.

2 In a large bowl with an electric mixer, beat cake mix, oil, eggs, and vanilla until thoroughly combined. Chill dough at least 45 minutes allowing it to firm up.

3 In a small bowl, combine sugar and cinnamon; mix well. Form dough into 1-inch balls, then roll in sugar mixture until evenly coated. Place on 2 ungreased baking sheets, about 2 inches apart, and flatten each cookie slightly using the bottom of a glass. [See Tip.]

4 Bake 7 to 9 minutes, or until golden. Let cool 5 minutes, then remove to a wire rack to cool completely. Store in an airtight container.

Test Kitchen Tip: *Are you wondering why we flatten the cookies with a glass? The reason is, if we use our hands, the cinnamon sugar will stick to them. Also, since the bottom of the glass is flat, it'll ensure that our cookies are perfectly flat, which will help them bake evenly.*

Nutty Fudge Dunkin' Crinkles

If there's one cookie in this book that's perfect for dunking, it's definitely this one. They've got the perfect consistency for "optimal dunkability" (that's our own food-science term), which basically means they're soft enough to absorb the right amount of milk, yet firm enough to withstand dip after dip. So hey, how about you get out a glass of your favorite milk and put these cookies to the test?

Makes 36 cookies

Ingredients

½ cup finely chopped almonds

2 tablespoons sugar

1 package gluten-free devil's food cake mix

1 (4-serving size) package gluten-free chocolate instant pudding mix

1 stick (½ cup) butter, melted

1 egg

⅓ cup water

1-½ teaspoons almond extract

Preparation

1 Preheat oven to 350 degrees F. In a shallow dish, combine almonds and sugar; set aside.

2 In a large bowl with an electric mixer, beat cake mix and pudding mix. Add butter, egg, water, and almond extract; beat until soft dough forms.

3 Shape dough into 1-inch balls; roll in almond and sugar mixture. Place on ungreased baking sheets, about 2 inches apart, and flatten slightly.

4 Bake 8 to 10 minutes, or until set. Cool 5 minutes, then remove to wire racks to cool completely. Store in an airtight container.

Did You Know? Although several brands of instant puddings are considered gluten-free, they may not always carry the gluten-free label. That's because they may have come into contact with gluten during the manufacturing process. So, if it's not marked as gluten-free, and that's important to you, then make sure you find one that is. And if gluten isn't an issue in your diet, then feel free to make this with standard ingredients.

GLUTEN FREE

Nonna's Shortcut Ricotta Cookies

Even the most old-school nonna (that's grandma in Italian!) turns to shortcuts from time to time, especially if she's got a whole lot of cooking ahead of her. The thing is, most of the time, no one can even tell she took a shortcut! That's the case with these almost-world-famous ricotta cookies, shared with us by a real nonna. They're good enough to become one of the most anticipated cookies on your Christmas cookie platter!

Makes 36 cookies

Ingredients

1 package white cake mix

1 cup ricotta cheese

½ stick [¼ cup] butter, melted

1 egg

1 teaspoon anise extract

¼ cup holiday nonpareils for decorating

GLAZE

2-½ cups confectioners' sugar

¼ cup milk

¼ teaspoon anise extract

Preparation

1 Preheat oven to 350 degrees F.

2 In a large bowl with an electric mixer, beat cake mix, ricotta cheese, butter, egg, and 1 teaspoon anise extract until thoroughly combined. Drop by heaping teaspoonfuls onto baking sheets, about 1 inch apart.

3 Bake 10 to 12 minutes, or until golden. Cool 5 minutes, then remove to a wire rack to cool completely.

4 To make glaze, in a medium bowl, whisk confectioners' sugar, milk and ¼ teaspoon anise extract, until smooth. Spoon glaze over cookies, then immediately decorate with nonpareils.

HOLIDAY SPECIAL

Chocolate-Dipped Berry-Nut Biscotti

Instead of paying top dollar at one of those high-end coffee houses for biscotti to dip into your gourmet coffee, you can make a whole batch of these for next to nothing. Serve these up the next time you've invited friends over to play some cards or a game of Mahjong and you'll be the talk of the block.

Makes 36 cookies

Ingredients

1 package white cake mix

1 (4-serving size) package cook and serve vanilla pudding mix

2 tablespoons vegetable oil

2 eggs, lightly beaten

1 cup flaked coconut, toasted

½ cup slivered almonds

¼ cup dried cranberries

1 cup semisweet chocolate chips

1 teaspoon shortening

Preparation

1 Preheat oven to 350 degrees F.

2 In a large bowl with an electric mixer, beat cake mix, pudding mix, oil, and eggs until thoroughly combined. Stir in coconut, almonds, and cranberries; mix well, using your hands, if necessary. On an ungreased baking sheet, form dough into a 15- x 4-inch rectangle, using greased hands.

3 Bake 25 to 30 minutes, or until golden. Cool 15 minutes.

4 Cut the rectangle crosswise into ½-inch slices. Place slices, cut-side down, on baking sheet. Bake 12 to 15 minutes longer, or until edges are golden brown. Cool 5 minutes; remove from baking sheet to a wire rack.

5 In a small microwave-safe bowl, combine chocolate chips and shortening. Microwave 60 to 90 seconds, stirring occasionally until smooth. Dip one end of each cookie in chocolate. Return to wire rack and let stand about 30 minutes, or until chocolate is set. Store in an airtight container.

Dangerously Delicious Stuffed Pizookie

How about, this weekend, you grab your cast iron skillet and whip up this stuffed skillet cookie, also known as a "pizookie"? A pizookie is basically a cross between a pizza and an oversized cookie, which means it's totally shareable and 100% perfect. And since we stuffed ours with everyone's favorite chocolate-hazelnut filling, you can bet that this one is dangerously delicious.

Serves 8

Ingredients

1 (17.5-ounce) package chocolate chip cookie mix

1 stick (½ cup) butter, softened

1 egg

1 tablespoon water

1 teaspoon vanilla extract

½ cup chocolate-hazelnut spread

Preparation

1 Preheat oven to 350 degrees F. Coat a 9-inch cast iron skillet with cooking spray.

2 In a large bowl, combine cookie mix, butter, egg, water, and vanilla; mix with a spoon until combined, using your hands if necessary. (Mixture will be stiff.) Press half the dough into skillet.

3 Evenly distribute chocolate-hazelnut spread over cookie dough. Top with remaining cookie dough and gently smooth with a wet knife to cover chocolate-hazelnut spread.

4 Bake 30 to 35 minutes, or until light golden and just firm in center. Let cool slightly and serve warm, or cool completely.

Note: If you don't have a cast iron skillet, you can make this in a 9-inch cake pan.

Serving Suggestion: Believe it or not, you can take this mouthwatering dessert a step further by serving with a scoop of vanilla ice cream and a drizzle of chocolate-hazelnut spread. There's no looking back now!

Dusted Zucchini Cookie Sticks

You might want to dog-ear the corner of this page, so when your garden begins to overflow with summer's best zucchini, you'll have this recipe at your fingertips. What we like about these is that they're crispy on the outside, but moist and flavorful on the inside. Oh, and if you're a cookie dunker, then you're really going to love these!

Makes 28 sticks

Ingredients

1 package spice cake mix

1 cup water

⅓ cup vegetable oil

3 eggs

1 teaspoon vanilla extract

1-½ cups shredded zucchini

¾ cup chopped walnuts

Confectioners' sugar for dusting

Preparation

1 Preheat oven to 350 degrees F. Coat 2 (9- x 5-inch) loaf pans with cooking spray.

2 In a large bowl with an electric mixer, beat cake mix, water, oil, eggs, and vanilla extract until thoroughly combined. Stir in zucchini and walnuts. Pour batter evenly into both loaf pans. (It will only fill them about 1/3 of the way, that's ok.)

3 Bake 40 to 45 minutes, or until a toothpick inserted in center comes out clean. Let cool 10 minutes, then remove to a wire rack to cool an additional 15 minutes. Cut each loaf into ¾-inch-thick slices. (The loaves will be very dense.) Place slices cut-side down on ungreased baking sheets.

4 Bake 10 minutes, then turn slices over and bake an additional 10 minutes, or until lightly crisp. Let cool. Dust with confectioners' sugar before serving. Store in an airtight container.

Classic Italian Rainbow Cookies

Go to any Italian bakery in the U.S. and, among the cannoli and biscotti, you're sure to spot these rainbow cookies. These tri-colored cookies are moist, almond-flavored, and feature layers of fruity jam. To finish them off, we top them with a layer of smooth chocolate. It doesn't get much better than that!

Makes 48 cookies

Ingredients

1 package yellow cake mix

1 cup water

⅓ cup plus ¼ teaspoon vegetable oil, divided

3 eggs

1-½ teaspoons almond extract

1 teaspoon red food color

1 teaspoon green food color

1 teaspoon yellow food color

1 cup seedless raspberry jam, divided

1 cup semisweet chocolate chips

Test Kitchen Tip: *To cut through chocolate without it cracking, run a sharp knife under hot water for 10 seconds. Dry the knife, then cut into bars.*

Preparation

1 Preheat oven to 325 degrees F. Coat 3 (9- x 13-inch) baking dishes with cooking spray, line with wax paper, and coat again with cooking spray.

2 In a large bowl with an electric mixer, beat cake mix, water, ⅓ cup oil, the eggs, and almond extract until thoroughly combined. Divide batter evenly into 3 small bowls. Stir red color into one bowl, green color into another bowl, and yellow color into the third bowl. Pour each batter evenly into a separate baking dish. (The layer of batter will be very thin.)

3 Bake 15 to 18 minutes, or until cakes are firm. Let cool completely.

4 Place red layer top-side down on a cutting board and remove wax paper. Spread ½ cup raspberry jam evenly over top, then place yellow layer top-side down over jam. Remove wax paper and spread remaining ½ cup jam over yellow layer. Place green layer on top, leaving wax paper in place. Place a baking sheet over the top layer and gently press the layers together. Chill 1 hour, then remove wax paper.

5 In a microwave-safe bowl, combine chocolate chips and remaining ¼ teaspoon oil. Microwave 60 to 90 seconds, stirring occasionally until smooth. Spread a thin layer over top of cake and allow to harden. Cut into 1- x 2-inch bars and chill until ready to serve.

Mixed Fruit Cookie Tart

Desserts like this one are real crowd-pleasers. Not only does this cookie tart, topped with all of your favorite fruits, look good, but it tastes amazing, too! A sugar cookie crust and a creamy layer of pudding really brings it all together. Serve up a slice and watch as their faces light up.

Serves 12

Ingredients

1 (17.5-ounce) package sugar cookie mix

1 stick (½ cup) butter, softened and cut into pieces

1 egg

2 teaspoons vanilla extract, divided

1 cup chopped walnuts

1 (4-serving size) package instant vanilla pudding mix

1 cup milk

1 cup frozen whipped topping, thawed

1 kiwi, peeled and sliced

1 orange, peeled and sectioned

1 cup strawberries, sliced

½ cup raspberries

½ cup blueberries

½ cup blackberries

Preparation

1 Preheat oven to 350 degrees F. Coat a 14-inch round pizza pan with cooking spray.

2 In a large bowl with an electric mixer, beat cookie mix, butter, egg, and 1 teaspoon vanilla until thoroughly combined. Stir in walnuts. Press dough into pan, leaving a 1-inch border.

3 Bake 18 to 20 minutes, or until light golden around edges and just set in center. Let cool completely.

4 In a medium bowl, whisk pudding mix, milk, and remaining 1 teaspoon vanilla until thickened. Stir in whipped topping until thoroughly combined. Spread evenly over cookie crust. Garnish with fruit, as shown.

So Many Options! You can easily change this tart every time by changing up the fruit. For example, in the fall you can top with cranberries and slices of apples or pears, while in the spring you can try a tropical variation with pineapple and mango chunks.

Diner-Style Black & White Cookies

We've come to the conclusion that there's a reason why so many diners have you pay your check near the bakery case at the front of the restaurant. It's because they know that once you get a glimpse of all the tempting desserts, you're bound to order some for the road. And one favorite that many of us have a hard time resisting are those black and white cookies, which reminds us...what side did you bite into first?

Makes 18 cookies

Ingredients

1 package chocolate cake mix

¼ cup vegetable oil

2 eggs

½ (16-ounce) container chocolate frosting

½ (16-ounce) container vanilla frosting

Preparation

1 Preheat oven to 350 degrees F. Coat two baking sheets with cooking spray.

2 In a large bowl with an electric mixer, beat cake mix, oil, and eggs until thoroughly combined. Drop by heaping tablespoonfuls 2 inches apart onto baking sheets. Bake 12 to 14 minutes, or until firm. Remove cookies to wire racks to cool completely.

3 Frost half of the flat side of each cookie with vanilla frosting and the other half with chocolate frosting. Store in an airtight container.

Test Kitchen Tip: *Since we only use half of each container of frosting, feel free to store the leftovers in the fridge until the next time you make a batch.*

Rocky Road Ice Cream Sandwiches

When the mercury on your thermometer begins to rise, you'll know it's time to whip up a batch of these old-fashioned ice cream sandwiches. And unlike traditional ice cream sandwiches, these are overstuffed with rocky road ice cream and fancied up with more chocolate and sliced almonds. So, grab a napkin and go to town!

Makes 8 sandwiches

Ingredients

1 package chocolate cake mix

⅓ cup vegetable oil

1 egg

½ gallon rocky road ice cream, slightly softened

½ cup mini chocolate chips

½ cup sliced almonds, finely chopped

Preparation

1 Preheat oven to 350 degrees F. Coat baking sheets with cooking spray.

2 In a large bowl with an electric mixer, beat cake mix, oil, and egg until thoroughly combined. Drop 16 heaping tablespoonfuls 2 inches apart on baking sheets. Bake 13 to 15 minutes, or until firm. Remove cookies to wire racks to cool completely.

3 Place a scoop of ice cream on flat side of a cookie; place another cookie, flat side down, on ice cream. Squeeze 2 cookies together until ice cream is pushed to the edges. Repeat with remaining cookies and ice cream.

4 Place chocolate chips on a plate; place almonds on another plate. Roll edges of ice cream sandwiches over the chips, then over the almonds. Place on a baking sheet and freeze. Once frozen hard, wrap each in plastic wrap and return to the freezer until ready to serve.

Mix 'n' Match: *If you're serving these at your next pool party, you might want to give your guests a few different flavor options. Maybe you can make half of them with rocky road ice cream and the other half with another one of your favorite ice cream flavors. You can also roll the edges in sprinkles, coconut flakes, or other types of nuts. The possibilities are endless!*

FROZEN TREAT

Almond Cookie Bark with Chocolate Lace

For lots of crispy crunchy goodness, all you've got to do is bake up our Almond Cookie Bark. Whether you break it into bite-sized pieces for nibbling on, or you grab yourself an extra-large piece for dunkin', there's no way you can go wrong.

Makes about 24 pieces

Ingredients

1 (17.5-ounce) package sugar cookie mix

1 stick (½ cup) butter, softened and cut into pieces

1 tablespoon water

1 teaspoon almond extract

¾ cup chopped almonds

½ cup semisweet chocolate chips

½ teaspoon vegetable oil

Preparation

1 Preheat oven to 350 degrees F. Coat a 10- x 15-inch rimmed baking sheet with cooking spray.

2 In a large bowl, combine cookie mix, butter, water, almond extract, and almonds; using your hands (see Tip), mix until thoroughly combined. (Mixture will be stiff.) Press dough into bottom of pan.

3 Bake 15 to 20 minutes, or until light golden. Let cool, then cut into triangle-shaped pieces.

4 In a small microwave-safe bowl, combine chocolate chips and oil. Microwave 60 to 75 seconds, stirring occasionally until smooth. With a fork, drizzle over cookies and allow to harden. Store in an airtight container.

Test Kitchen Tip: *The reason we think it's best to mix this with our hands is because the warmth from our hands keeps the butter at the perfect temperature, and allows all the nutty goodness to mix in evenly.*

A Little of This,
A Little of That

Apple 'n' Spice Pull-Apart Bread

When we first taste-tested this recipe in the Test Kitchen, we practically had to form a single file line so everyone could get a chance to pull apart their piece. Once someone got a bite, it was hard to keep them from finishing the whole dessert on their own! All kidding aside, this may just be one of the best recipes we've ever created. Try it and let us know what you think on Facebook!

Serves 8

Ingredients

1 round loaf hearty white or sourdough bread, unsliced

1-½ sticks (¾ cup) butter, melted

½ cup spice cake mix

½ cup light brown sugar

1 apple, peeled, cored, and finely diced

1 cup confectioners' sugar

1 tablespoon milk

Preparation

1 Preheat oven to 350 degrees F. Coat a baking sheet with cooking spray. Using a serrated knife, make a crisscross pattern in the bread, slicing 1 inch apart, cutting almost all the way to the bottom but being careful not to cut through completely. Place bread on baking sheet. Evenly drizzle butter between each bread section.

2 In a medium bowl, combine dry cake mix and brown sugar; mix well. Add apples and toss until evenly coated. Evenly sprinkle the apple mixture between each of the bread sections, being careful not to break bread apart. Sprinkle any remaining mixture over the bread. Bake 25 to 30 minutes, or until bread is crispy.

3 In a small bowl, whisk confectioners' sugar and milk until smooth. Drizzle over warm bread and serve immediately.

Test Kitchen Tip: *Since you won't be using up a whole box of cake mix in this recipe, make sure you store any leftover mix in an airtight container.*

Old-Fashioned Pound Cake

Our way of making an old-fashioned pound cake is certainly a lot simpler than when it was first created in the mid-18th century. No need to measure out a pound of this and a pound of that (hence its name!). With our version all you have to do is mix, bake, and enjoy. The best part? We still get all that rich, buttery taste that everyone expects!

Serves 10

Ingredients

1 package yellow cake mix

1 (4-serving size) package instant vanilla pudding mix

1 cup water

1 stick (½ cup) butter, melted

4 eggs

2 teaspoons vanilla extract

Preparation

1 Preheat oven to 350 degrees F. Coat a 9- x 5-inch loaf pan with cooking spray.

2 In a large bowl with an electric mixer, beat all ingredients until thoroughly combined. Pour into loaf pan.

3 Bake 50 to 55 minutes, or until a toothpick inserted in center comes out clean. Let cool 20 minutes, then invert onto a wire rack to cool completely.

Finishing Touch: *Go from simple to amazing by topping each slice with your own homemade vanilla whipped cream. In a medium bowl with an electric mixer, beat 1 cup heavy cream for 1 minute. Add 1 tablespoon sugar and 1 tablespoon vanilla; continue beating 3 to 4 more minutes, or until stiff peaks form.*

Heart-Shaped Cupid's Cake

Nothing says "I love you" quite like this heart-shaped cake. Whether you're making it for Valentine's Day, to celebrate a special anniversary, or "just because," this cake is sure to leave them feeling like they've been struck by Cupid's arrow. After all, how could anyone resist falling in love over a moist, red velvet cake topped with a cheesecake-flavored, whipped cream frosting? Oh yeah, we know how to sweeten your sweetie.

Serves 16

Ingredients

1 package red velvet cake mix

1 (4-serving size) package instant chocolate pudding mix

2 cups milk, divided

⅓ cup vegetable oil

3 eggs

1 (4-serving size) package instant cheesecake pudding mix

1 (8-ounce) container frozen whipped topping, thawed

Preparation

1 Preheat oven to 350 degrees F. Coat one (8-inch) square baking pan and one (8-inch) round baking pan with cooking spray.

2 In a large bowl with an electric mixer, beat cake mix, chocolate pudding mix, 1 cup milk, the oil, and eggs until thoroughly combined. Pour batter evenly into baking pans. Bake 28 to 32 minutes, or until a toothpick inserted in center comes out clean. Let cool 10 minutes, then remove to a wire rack to cool completely.

3 Place square cake toward bottom of a large platter, positioning it like a diamond. Cut round cake in half, creating two half circles, then place halves on platter with flat sides flush to the top right and top left sides of the "diamond". This will create a heart shape. Using a serrated knife, trim tops of cakes so they're flat, and reserve excess pieces to crumble for garnish.

4 In a large bowl, whisk cheesecake pudding mix with remaining 1 cup milk until slightly thickened. Gently stir in whipped topping until well combined. Refrigerate 30 minutes, or until thickened.

5 Frost top and sides of cake. Garnish with excess cake crumbs. Keep refrigerated.

HOLIDAY SPECIAL

Honey Pecan Coffee Cake

The next time you've got guests coming over for breakfast or brunch, we suggest you make this company-special coffee cake. It's loaded (like, really loaded!) with pecans, which add a nutty crunch to every forkful. Plus, we sweetened our cake with a combination of brown sugar and honey, so there's a homestyle taste that everyone will enjoy. In short, it's a cake that's just as special as your guests.

Serves 8

Ingredients

5 tablespoons butter

¼ cup light brown sugar

¾ cup honey, divided

2 teaspoons vanilla extract, divided

1-¼ cups pecan halves

1 package yellow cake mix

1 cup water

⅓ cup vegetable oil

3 eggs

Preparation

1 Preheat oven to 350 degrees F. Coat bottom and sides of a 10-inch springform pan with cooking spray and line bottom with wax paper; set aside.

2 In a small saucepan over medium heat, melt butter, brown sugar, and ¼ cup honey. Bring to a boil, remove from heat, and stir in 1 teaspoon vanilla and the pecans. Pour mixture into bottom of pan; set aside.

3 In a large bowl with an electric mixer, beat cake mix, water, oil, eggs, the remaining ½ cup honey, and the remaining 1 teaspoon vanilla until thoroughly combined. Pour batter evenly over nut mixture.

4 Bake 45 to 50 minutes, or until a toothpickinserted in center comes out clean; let cool. Remove outer ring of pan, invert cake onto platter, and remove bottom of pan and wax paper.

Test Kitchen Tip: *The best way to remove the cake from the springform pan is to place the pan on a soup bowl, unlatch the clip and let the ring drop to the counter. Yes, it's that easy!*

Chocolate Frosted Sour Cream Donuts

We can't think of a sweeter way to start your morning than with one of our freshly baked sour cream donuts. These are especially great to make with the kids or grandkids, since everyone can decorate their own. Serve with a glass of cold milk and they'll be all smiles!

Makes 18

Ingredients

1 package yellow cake mix

1 cup water

½ cup sour cream

¼ cup vegetable oil

1 egg

1 teaspoon vanilla extract

1 (16-ounce) container chocolate frosting

Sprinkles for garnish

Preparation

1 Preheat oven to 350 degrees F. Coat donut pans (see Tip) with cooking spray.

2 In a large bowl with an electric mixer, beat cake mix, water, sour cream, oil, egg, and vanilla until thoroughly combined. Spoon batter evenly into donut pans, filling each well halfway.

3 Bake 12 to 15 minutes, or until golden. Let cool 5 minutes, then remove to wire racks to cool completely. Repeat with remaining batter, if necessary. Spread frosting on top of donuts and garnish with sprinkles.

Test Kitchen Tip: *"Donut worry!" You can find inexpensive donut pans at most big-box retailers. And if you don't have enough pans to make 18 donuts at a time, you may have to wait for your first batch to come out of the oven and cool before baking another tray or two.*

Apple Cider Baked Donuts

If you've ever gone apple picking or taken a hayride, then there's a pretty good chance that you've had apple cider donuts. It's a fall thing that once experienced, is sort of hard to forget about. Luckily, you don't have to wait until your next visit to the orchard to enjoy this treat, since our recipe is so easy and can be made anytime of the year.

Makes 18

Ingredients

1 package yellow cake mix

1 cup apple cider or juice

½ cup sour cream

¼ cup vegetable oil

1 egg

½ teaspoon ground cinnamon, divided

¼ teaspoon ground nutmeg

¼ cup confectioners' sugar

Preparation

1 Preheat oven to 350 degrees F. Coat donut pans with cooking spray. (see Tip, page 238)

2 In a large bowl with an electric mixer, beat cake mix, cider, sour cream, oil, egg, ¼ teaspoon cinnamon, and the nutmeg until thoroughly combined. Spoon batter evenly into donut pans, filling each well halfway.

3 Bake 12 to 15 minutes, or until golden. Let cool 5 minutes, then remove to wire racks to cool completely. Repeat with remaining batter, if necessary.

4 In a small bowl, combine confectioners' sugar and remaining ¼ teaspoon cinnamon; mix well. Sprinkle evenly on donuts.

Serving Suggestion: *We like to enjoy these with mugs of apple cider. Just warm up your cider, add in a cinnamon stick, and you've got the perfect sipper!*

Pumpkin Cheesecake Overstuffed Whoopie Pies

We may have gotten a little carried away with how much filling we put into these, but you can't blame us for wanting to pack as much fall flavor into every bite as we could. Besides, now you can find out whether you're the kind of person who eats this one bite at a time or the kind that smushes the cake part together, so you can lick the cheesecake filling first. Don't worry; we're not judging either way!

Makes 18

Ingredients

1 package spice cake mix

1 (15-ounce) can pure pumpkin (not pumpkin pie filling)

¼ cup vegetable oil

1-½ teaspoons vanilla extract, divided

1 (4-serving size) package instant cheesecake pudding mix

2 cups (1 pint) heavy cream

Preparation

1 Preheat oven to 350 degrees F. Coat baking sheets with cooking spray.

2 In a large bowl with an electric mixer, beat cake mix, pumpkin, oil, and 1 teaspoon vanilla until thoroughly combined. Using a small ice cream scoop or a large soup spoon place 36 scoops of dough on baking sheets.

3 Bake 15 to 18 minutes, or until a toothpick comes out clean. Let cool 5 minutes, then remove to a wire rack to cool completely.

4 In a medium bowl with an electric mixer, beat pudding, heavy cream, and remaining ½ teaspoon vanilla until stiff. Dollop or pipe the filling evenly onto flat side of half the cookies. Place remaining cookies flat side down over filling to form overstuffed sandwiches, pressing together lightly. Keep refrigerated.

Red Velvet Whoopie Pies

Legend has it that this fun treat got its name from the children who would shout "Whoopie!" when they discovered one packed inside their lunch boxes. And this is the same reaction you'll get when you set out a platter stacked high with our red velvet version. Filled with a fluffy marshmallow crème filling, this sandwich-style treat has come a long way since its traditional Amish origins.

Makes 12

Ingredients

1 package red velvet cake mix

2 eggs

¼ cup vegetable oil

¼ cup water

2 cups marshmallow crème

1-½ sticks [¾ cup] butter, softened

1 teaspoon vanilla extract

2 cups confectioners' sugar

Preparation

1 Preheat oven to 350 degrees F. Coat baking sheets with cooking spray.

2 In a large bowl with an electric mixer, beat cake mix, eggs, oil, and water until thoroughly combined. Drop 24 heaping teaspoons of batter onto baking sheets 2 inches apart. Bake 10 to 15 minutes, or until a toothpick comes out clean. Let cool 5 minutes, then remove to a wire rack to cool completely.

3 In a medium bowl with an electric mixer, beat marshmallow crème, butter, and vanilla until creamy. Slowly add confectioners' sugar and beat until smooth. Place a dollop of filling evenly onto flat side of half the cookies. Place remaining cookies flat side down over filling to form sandwiches, pressing together lightly. Keep refrigerated.

Did You Know? *In 2011, Maine declared the whoopie pie the official state treat. The state even hosts an annual whoopie pie festival to celebrate their love for this dessert.*

Chocolate Waffle Sundaes With Raspberry Sauce

If your taste buds get excited just thinking about a hot fudge sundae, there's no telling what'll happen once they get a taste of these hot-off-the-griddle chocolate waffles smothered in raspberry sauce, topped with vanilla ice cream, and laced with hot fudge. You better fasten your seatbelt for this one!

Serves 6

Ingredients

1 (12-ounce) package frozen raspberries

½ cup sugar

1 cup plus 4 tablespoons water, divided

1 tablespoon cornstarch

1 package devil's food cake mix

⅓ cup vegetable oil

3 eggs

1 quart vanilla ice cream

½ cup hot fudge

Preparation

1 In a medium saucepan over medium heat, combine raspberries, sugar, and 2 tablespoons water. Cook 6 to 8 minutes, or until berries have broken down. In a small bowl, whisk cornstarch and 2 tablespoons water. Whisk mixture into raspberries and continue to cook until thickened. Pour into a bowl and cool.

2 Meanwhile, preheat waffle maker until hot.

3 In a large bowl with an electric mixer, beat cake mix, remaining 1 cup water, the oil, and eggs until thoroughly combined.

4 Coat waffle maker with cooking spray. Pour 1/3 cup batter onto waffle maker, close lid, and cook 3 to 5 minutes, or until waffle is set. Remove to a platter, cover to keep warm, and repeat with remaining batter. Top waffles with raspberry sauce, ice cream, and hot fudge. Serve immediately.

Test Kitchen Tip: *Since waffle irons vary in size, always check your owner's manual to see how much batter is recommended to use. It may take a waffle or two before you get it just perfect, but once you do…oh boy!*

Autumn-Spiced Pumpkin Pancakes

The smell of these pancakes cooking on the griddle is enough to make you dream of rust-colored leaves, cozy autumn days, and crisp fall nights. But just because pumpkin season doesn't officially start until September doesn't mean you have to wait to fill your home with that sweet, spiced pumpkin smell. Our pancakes can be made any time. Slather on some butter and real maple syrup and you're on track to having the best morning ever.

Makes 18 to 20 pancakes

Ingredients

1 package spice cake mix

½ cup canned pure pumpkin (not pumpkin pie filling)

¼ teaspoon ground cinnamon

1-¼ cups milk

⅓ cup vegetable oil

2 eggs

Butter for melting

Preparation

1 In a large bowl, whisk cake mix, pumpkin, cinnamon, milk, oil, and eggs until thoroughly combined and smooth.

2 In a skillet or griddle over medium-low heat, melt 1 tablespoon butter. Pour about ⅓ cup batter per pancake onto skillet, being sure not to overcrowd. When bubbles form on top, flip pancakes and cook 1 minute, or until golden. Repeat with remaining batter, adding more butter as needed.

Over-the-Rainbow Pudding Parfaits

You might not find a pot of gold at the end of this rainbow, but you will find lots of creamy pudding and crispy cookie crumbs in every spoonful. It's so good, you'll be digging in to get every last bit out of the glass. The colorful look is just a bonus. So, what are you waiting for? It's time to bake a rainbow!

Serves 5

Ingredients

1 (17.5-ounce) package sugar cookie mix

1 stick (½ cup) butter, softened

1 egg

20 drops each red, green, blue, and yellow food color

1 (4-serving size) package instant vanilla pudding mix

1-¼ cups milk

2 cups frozen whipped topping, thawed

Preparation

1 Preheat oven to 350 degrees F. Coat 2 baking sheets with cooking spray.

2 In a large bowl, combine cookie mix, butter, and egg; mix well with a large spoon until it becomes a soft dough. Divide dough evenly into 4 small bowls. Add 20 drops of red food color to one bowl of dough, stirring with a spoon or kneading with your hands until thoroughly combined. Repeat with remaining food colors and dough. Place 2 dough balls on each baking sheet about 3 inches apart. (Dough will spread.) Bake 10 to 12 minutes, or until light golden around edges. Let cool 5 minutes, then remove to a wire rack to cool completely.

3 In a large bowl, whisk pudding mix and milk until thickened. Stir in whipped topping until thoroughly combined.

4 Crumble the cookies into bowls, keeping the colors separate.

5 Evenly spoon one cookie color into the bottom of 5 juice glasses. Top with a spoonful of pudding. Repeat with remaining colors and the pudding, creating colorful layers as shown. Keep refrigerated.

Test Kitchen Tip: *How much pudding and cookies you will need for each layer depends on the size of your glasses.*

Fresh 'n' Fruity Cheesecake Bites

Some people might prefer to eat these with a fork, one bite at a time, while others would rather enjoy them as one-bite treats. The good news is, there's no right or wrong way to go about it! What makes these so unique is how the cake mix lightens up the cheesecake filling. And when you top them with your favorite combo of fresh fruit, you've got a winning dessert that's great for entertaining!

Serves 12

Ingredients

1 cup graham cracker crumbs

¼ cup plus 2 tablespoons sugar, divided

½ stick (¼ cup) butter, melted

1 (8-ounce) package cream cheese, softened

3 tablespoons sour cream

1 egg

1 teaspoon vanilla extract

½ cup white cake mix

Assorted fresh fruit for garnish

2 tablespoons apple jelly, melted

Preparation

1 Preheat oven to 350 degrees F. Place paper liners in 12 muffin cups.

2 In a medium bowl, combine cracker crumbs, 2 tablespoons sugar, and the butter; mix well. Place 1-½ tablespoons crumb mixture into bottom of each paper liner and press down.

3 In a large bowl with an electric mixer, beat cream cheese, sour cream, egg, and vanilla until creamy. Add cake mix and remaining ¼ cup sugar and mix until smooth. Divide batter evenly between muffin cups.

4 Bake 15 to 18 minutes, or just until set. Let cool completely, then refrigerate. Before serving, garnish with fruit and brush with jelly. Keep refrigerated.

Yummy Mummy Cake Pops

Instead of keeping this recipe "under wraps" we've decided to share it with you, so you can serve these at your next Halloween party. Not only are they super easy to make and bring along, but they're devilishly good and perfectly themed. All the little ghouls and goblins will love these - oh, and their mummies, too!

Makes 24

Ingredients

1 package white cake mix, baked according to package directions for a 9- x 13-inch baking dish, and cooled

¾ cup white frosting

24 (6-inch) cake pop or lollipop sticks

2 (10-ounce) bags white candy melting discs

48 mini chocolate chips

Preparation

1 Line 2 baking sheets with wax paper.

2 After cake has cooled, using your hands or a food processor, crumble the cake into fine crumbs. Add the frosting and mix (almost knead) with your hands until thoroughly combined. Form mixture into 24 pear-shaped balls (see photo) and place on baking sheets. Gently place a cake pop stick about 1-inch into the narrow end of each cake ball. Cover and refrigerate 1 hour.

3 In a large microwave-safe bowl, microwave candy discs 60 seconds. Stir, then continue to microwave at 15 second intervals, until melted and smooth. (Do not overheat.)

4 Holding each cake pop stick over the melted candy, spoon melted candy over entire cake pop, allowing excess to drip off. Return to baking sheet. Repeat until all cake pops are coated, then refrigerate until coating is hardened.

5 Reheat remaining candy coating until melted. Place in a resealable plastic bag, cut tip off of one corner; drizzle over pops in a zig-zag pattern. Secure mini chocolate chips onto each mummy to create eyes using the melted candy discs as glue.

Sweet 'n' Salty Popcorn Mix

Just when we thought a bowl of popcorn couldn't get any better, we surprised ourselves by coming up with this ooey-gooey popcorn mix. This mix features a salty kick from your favorite nuts and a sweet touch from the marshmallows, vanilla, and (our secret ingredient) cake mix. Whether you make this for movie night or for snack time, it's bound to be an empty-bowl success!

Serves 6

Ingredients

2 tablespoons butter

3 cups marshmallows

1 tablespoon milk

1 teaspoon vanilla extract

1 cup white cake mix

8 cups popped popcorn

1 cup mixed nuts

Preparation

1 In a large pot over medium-low heat, melt butter and marshmallows, stirring constantly until smooth.

2 Remove from heat and stir in milk, vanilla, and cake mix. Add popcorn and nuts, and mix until evenly coated. Let cool, then serve.

Test Kitchen Tip: *Make sure you store your leftover cake mix in an airtight container, so it's fresh and ready for your next batch of popcorn mix!*

Super Snackin' Puppy Chow

Don't you go thinking that you can feed this to your puppy! This popular snack food was nicknamed "puppy chow" because it looks like something that you might feed your puppy, but it's really only people-approved. Our puppy chow is perfect for anyone who loves nibbling on sweet and salty treats that crunch. It's a great snack to keep on hand for those times when you need a little energy boost.

Makes about 8 cups

Ingredients

3 cups oven-toasted corn cereal

3 cups mini twist pretzels

1 cup dried cranberries

1 cup candy-coated chocolates

½ cup white cake mix

¼ cup confectioners' sugar

½ (16-ounce) package vanilla almond bark

Preparation

1 Line a 10- x 15-inch baking sheet with wax paper.

2 In a large bowl, combine cereal, pretzels, cranberries, and candy-coated chocolates; mix well and set aside. In a small bowl, combine cake mix with confectioners' sugar.

3 In a medium microwave-safe bowl, melt almond bark 60 to 90 seconds, or until melted, stirring occasionally. Pour over cereal mixture and toss until evenly coated. Sprinkle with cake mix mixture and toss again. Place on baking sheet and let cool. Store in an airtight container.

Potato Stick Chocolate Fudge

There's nothing like walking into an old-fashioned fudge shop and taking in all of the varieties of fudge that are available. We've seen everything from traditional flavors, like vanilla and peanut butter, to out-of-the-ordinary flavors, like jelly bean and salted caramel. And one that Patty came across, and loved, was a chocolate and potato stick version that she described as "dee-loshus". We know you're going to love her fuss-free version.

Makes 25 pieces

Ingredients

2 cups chocolate cake mix

2 cups confectioners' sugar

1 stick (½ cup) butter, cut into 4 chunks

¼ cup milk

¾ cup semisweet chocolate chips

1 teaspoon vanilla extract

1-½ cups potato sticks, divided

Preparation

1 Coat an 8-inch square baking dish with cooking spray.

2 In a large microwave-safe bowl, combine cake mix and confectioners' sugar; mix well. Add butter and milk; do not stir.

3 Microwave 1-½ to 2 minutes, then stir until thoroughly combined. Stir in chocolate chips and vanilla until well blended. Add 1 cup potato sticks; mix well.

4 Spread fudge evenly in baking dish. Sprinkle with remaining ½ cup potato sticks and gently press into fudge. Refrigerate 2 hours, or until firm. Cut into squares. Keep refrigerated.

HOLIDAY SPECIAL

Big Island Macadamia Nut Fudge

Hawaii is famous for many of our favorite tropical treats - pineapples, coconuts, and...macadamia nuts! In fact, the Big Island of Hawaii is one of the largest producers of this buttery-tasting nut. So, to come up with this inspired fudge recipe, we put on our grass skirts and flowered leis and got to work. The result? An easy fudge that's melt-in-your-mouth good and loaded with lots of macadamia nuts. You'll be saying "aloha" to great taste in no time at all!

Makes 25 pieces

Ingredients

2 cups white cake mix

2 cups confectioners' sugar

1 stick (½ cup) butter, cut into 4 chunks

¼ cup milk

¾ cup white baking chips

1 teaspoon vanilla extract

1 (4.5-ounce) can macadamia nuts, coarsely chopped

Preparation

1 Coat an 8-inch square baking dish with cooking spray.

2 In a large microwave-safe bowl, combine cake mix and confectioners' sugar; mix well. Add butter and milk; do not stir.

3 Microwave 2 minutes, then stir until thoroughly combined. Stir in chips and vanilla until well blended. Add half the nuts; mix well.

4 Spread fudge evenly in baking dish. Sprinkle with remaining nuts and gently press into fudge. Refrigerate 2 hours, or until firm. Cut into squares. Keep refrigerated.

Test Kitchen Tip: *An average box of cake mix yields about 4 cups of dry mix. That means that one box will allow you to make this recipe twice. Isn't that great?!*

Chocolate-Dipped Pretzel Rods

Have you ever noticed just how expensive chocolate-dipped pretzels are in gourmet candy stores? Well, we did, and that was all the inspiration we needed to create this better-than-gourmet specialty. The fact that we can decorate them with all of our favorite candies makes them even more fun!

Makes about 2-½ dozen

Ingredients

1 (16-ounce) package chocolate almond bark

1 cup white cake mix, divided

1 (16-ounce) package vanilla almond bark

1 (12-ounce) package large pretzel rods

Assorted colored sprinkles for garnish

Assorted candies, chopped for garnish (See Note)

Preparation

1 Line 2 baking sheets with wax paper.

2 In a large microwave-safe bowl, melt chocolate almond bark in microwave 1-½ to 2 minutes, or until melted, stirring occasionally. (Do not overheat.) Stir in ½ cup cake mix; set aside. In another large microwave-safe bowl, repeat same process with vanilla almond bark and remaining cake mix.

3 Holding each pretzel rod by the top, spoon and spread melted chocolate over bottom two-thirds, allowing any excess chocolate to drip off. Immediately sprinkle chocolate-dipped pretzels with sprinkles or candy and place on baking sheet. Repeat with remaining pretzels, decorating as desired.

4 Chill 10 minutes, or until chocolate is set. Store in airtight containers.

NOTE: In the Test Kitchen, we used crushed Butterfingers®, mini M&M's®, and sprinkles.

Did You Know? *Almond bark is a candy coating confection, typically available in vanilla and chocolate flavors. Surprisingly, it's not actually made with any almonds at all, and it's unclear as to where the name comes from. You can find almond bark in the baking aisle near the other chocolate chips, and it's usually available in the form of blocks or discs.*

Vanilla Lovers' Cupcake Milkshake

Take a moment to think of all the flavors of ice cream you've seen in the freezer aisle or on the menu board at your local ice cream shop. (There are a lot aren't there?) Now, try to guess which one of those creative flavors is America's favorite...Did you guess vanilla? If so, you're correct! Classic vanilla is still the most requested flavor across the country, and we're celebrating its deliciousness with an unbelievably good, all-vanilla, jazzed-up milkshake.

Serves 2

Ingredients

2 frosted vanilla cupcakes (see Note)

4 large scoops vanilla ice cream

3 tablespoons vanilla frosting, divided

⅓ cup white cake mix

½ cup milk

3 tablespoons colored sprinkles

Preparation

1 Cut the top off of both cupcakes; set aside. Cut bottom of cupcakes into ½-inch chunks.

2 In a blender, combine ice cream, 2 tablespoons frosting, the cake mix, and milk; blend until smooth.

3 Evenly spread the remaining 1 tablespoon of frosting around the rim of 2 large mason jars or drinking glasses. Then, place sprinkles on a saucer and dip rims into sprinkles.

4 Place cupcake chunks in jars and pour milkshake over chunks, coating them. Garnish each jar with the frosted cupcake tops and more sprinkles. Serve immediately.

Note: As for the cupcakes, these can be store-bought or homemade.

Fancy It Up: To add even more pizzazz, you can add a little whipped cream on top.

Creamy Vanilla Caketini

There are lots of different ways to order a martini - on the rocks, dry, shaken, stirred...with cake. That's right, thanks to the availability of so many specialty-flavored vodkas, you can now make your favorite drink taste like your favorite dessert! This adults-only recipe is going to give a whole new meaning to your happy hour.

Serves 2

Ingredients

¼ cup cake-flavored vodka (see Note)

½ cup heavy cream

2 tablespoons vanilla cake mix

Decorative sugar (see note)

Whipped cream for garnish

Preparation

1 Fill a drink shaker or a 2-cup plastic container halfway with ice. Add vodka, heavy cream, and cake mix. Place top on and shake 15 seconds.

2 Pour drink mixture without the ice into sugar-rimmed cocktail glasses. (see Tip) Top with whipped cream and serve.

Note: Feel free to use whatever vodka you have on hand. Sure, plain will work fine, but the dessert flavors add a special touch.

Test Kitchen Tip: *To sugarcoat the rims of your glasses, place about a 1/4 cup of water on a small plate and sugar on another plate. Dip the rims of the glasses in the water and then into the sugar. Allow to set up a few minutes before serving.*

Dreamy Creamy Chocolate Buttercream

We think everyone will agree that if the frosting on a cake or cupcake isn't great, then why even bother? That's why we wanted to share a super creamy, super rich, buttercream frosting that's perfect for slathering on just about any dessert. We've even eaten it right out of the bowl with our fingers.

Makes 2-½ cups

Ingredients

1 stick (½ cup) butter, softened

½ cup half-and-half

1 teaspoon vanilla extract

1 pinch salt

4 cups confectioners' sugar

½ cup unsweetened cocoa powder

Preparation

1 In a large bowl with an electric mixer, beat butter, half-and-half, vanilla, and salt until thoroughly combined. Slowly beat in the confectioners' sugar until combined. Add cocoa powder and beat until light and creamy. Keep refrigerated. Bring to room temperature when ready to use.

Test Kitchen Tip: *If the frosting is a bit too stiff to spread, add a little bit more half-and-half, until frosting reaches spreading consistency. Just remember, add only a very little bit at a time. You can always add more, but you can't take it out.*

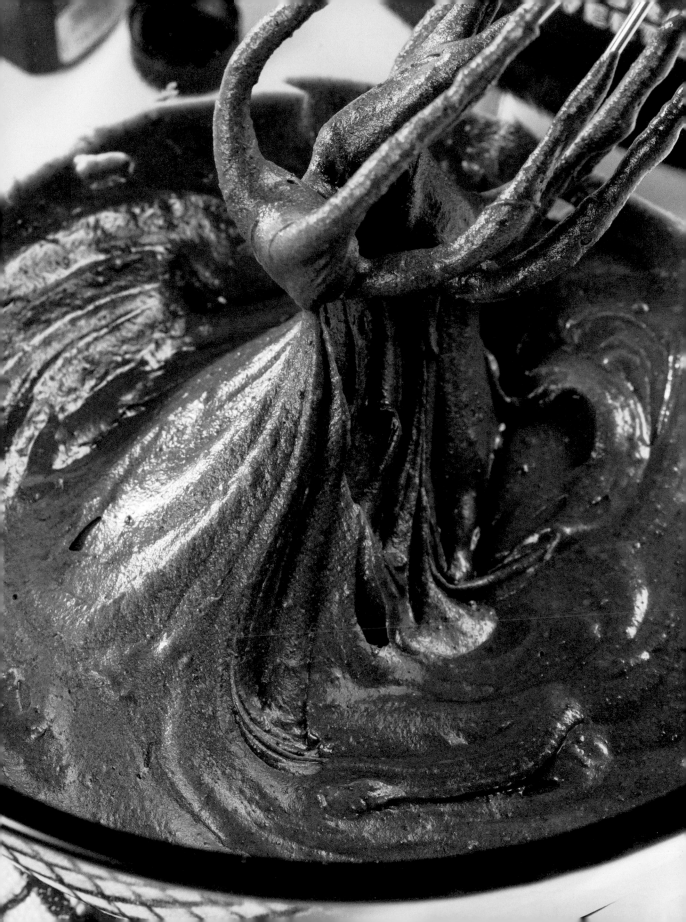

Fluffy Marshmallow Frosting

This is our fluffiest frosting yet! Made with everyone's favorite marshmallow crème, this creamy and sweet frosting adds a delightful flavor to all of your favorite desserts.

Makes 3-½ cups

Ingredients

1-¼ cups marshmallow crème

4 ounces cream cheese, softened

4 cups confectioners' sugar

¼ teaspoon ground cinnamon

1 teaspoon vanilla extract

Preparation

1 In a large bowl with an electric mixer, beat marshmallow crème and cream cheese until smooth. Slowly add in confectioners' sugar, cinnamon, and vanilla, and beat until thoroughly combined. Keep refrigerated. Bring to room temperature when ready to use.

Chocolate Hazelnut Buttercream

Okay, we'll confess. We may have stocked up on some extra chocolate hazelnut spread after finishing our recipes for Chocolate Hazelnut Crumb Cake (page 152) and Dangerously Delicious Stuffed Pizookie (page 210). But if we hadn't, this amazing frosting may never have come to be. Give it a try and you'll understand why we're not even sorry about it.

Makes 3 cups

Ingredients

1-½ sticks (¾ cup) butter, softened

1 cup chocolate hazelnut spread

1 tablespoon cocoa powder

1 teaspoon vanilla extract

3 cups confectioners' sugar

2 tablespoons milk

Preparation

1 In a large bowl with an electric mixer, beat butter, chocolate hazelnut spread, cocoa powder, and vanilla until creamy. Slowly add in confectioners' sugar and milk until smooth. Keep refrigerated. Bring to room temperature when ready to use.

Index